Global Goals for Societal

Volume II: Driving Education Towards the SDGs

Seema Goyal

walnutpublication.com

INDIA • UK • USA

Paperback ISBN: 979-8-89171-214-0
eBook ISBN: 979-8-89171-215-7

This book has been published following reasonable efforts to ensure the material is free from errors, with the author's full consent.
The publisher does not endorse or guarantee the accuracy, reliability, or completeness of the Content and expressly disclaims any liability for errors or omissions. No warranties of any kind are made, whether express or implied, including but not limited to warranties of merchantability or fitness for a particular purpose, or that the Content constitutes educational or medical advice.

First Published in May, 2025

Published by Walnut Publication

(an imprint of Vyusta Platforms Private Limited)

www.walnutpublication.com

India

Unit# 909, 9th Floor, Wave Silver Tower, Sector-18, Noida - 201301

UK

71-75 Shelton Street, Covent Garden, London, WC2H 9JQ, UK

Distributed by

ZopioTail

This Book is Dedicated to All of You

Acknowledgment

This book is the product of countless conversations, collaborations, and collective insights — and it would not have been possible without the support of many individuals and institutions.

First and foremost, I express my deepest gratitude to all the educators, researchers, and policy leaders whose dedication to Sustainable development and social equity continues to inspire this work. Your vision, scholarship, and perseverance laid the foundation for this inquiry.

Thank you for your guidance, your patience, and your unwavering belief in this project. Your insights challenged me to think more deeply and write more clearly.

To the communities, organizations, and field practitioners who generously shared their experiences and time — your stories gave this book its purpose and direction.

To my family and friends, thank you for your encouragement, emotional strength, and the many quiet sacrifices that allowed this work to take shape.

Our many thanks to every reader and changemaker committed to turning Global goals into local action. It is our hope that this work serves not just as a reference, but as a catalyst for continued dialogue, innovation, and transformation.

Finally, I acknowledge the many unsung contributors across sectors — educators in classrooms, students in discussion, policy advocates in negotiation rooms — who work daily to bring the Sustainable Development Goals from vision to reality.

About the Author

Seema Goyal

Educationist | SDG Advocate | Interdisciplinary Researcher | Sustainability Consultant | Founder of SDG Readiness Platform.

Seema Goyal, an Interdisciplinary researcher on SDGs in terms of Education, business and policy making, eager to reimagine the future as a more socially and environmentally just world, committed towards achieving the SDGs. With 20+ years-experience in curriculum design and assess Education sector policies, strategies and programs with a view of ensuring comparability to International best practices, smart solutions and technological advances, and responsiveness to development needs of the country.

We see the purpose of SDG Readiness Platform, as being a catalyst for change that will have an impact. It is a Platform working on SDG's and Climate crisis and aims to leave behind a legacy to inspire people and various stakeholders in this arena about solutions.

Our mission is to get the leaders to meet and learn from each other and be inspired by each other. We want to get this awareness out to millions. This is more than a book, a series of pro-planet book written for everyone –wherever you might be in the world. It is for those who want to easily understand how Climate Change is affecting the planet and who want to make small, simple changes in their everyday lives to become climate aware.

By sharing knowledge, leading by example, and creating spaces for conversation, I've found that I can engage others in meaningful discussions about sustainability. It's a journey that doesn't just involve personal commitment but also empowering others to understand how their actions, whether big or small, can contribute to a more Sustainable world.

Gandhi told us to 'be the change we want to see in the world.' This book captures that spirit, reminding us that everyone can do something to help the planet."

Preface

This Volume will explore the critical role of Education in shaping a more just and equitable world. It will offer an innovative perspective on how Education can be transformed to address the pressing social, economic, political, and ecological crisis and challenges of our time. Responding to growing interest in the Sustainable Development Goals (SDGs) and Global concern over Climate Change, this volume provides an analysis of how our understanding of the relationship between environment and Education has to evolve in the future –

Education for Societal Transformation: Through SDG's -an alternative for a just future

Proposing a set of key considerations for the future of Education, this book will be of value to scholars, researchers, policymakers, educators and practitioners working within sustainability Education, environmental research and policy, and teacher Education more broadly.

Anchored, as we are, in the UN Decade of Action, a suggested major goal of Education and learning is to contribute to accelerating the transformations needed to reach the 17 Sustainable Development Goals (SDGs) of Agenda 2030. This involves, among others, quality Education for all, decent work, clean water, health and well-being, zero hunger and no poverty, as well as climate action and strong institutions.

While it is clear that Education and learning has a fundamental role to play in establishing a more just relationship with ourselves, other species, and the planet as a whole, 50 years of policy, diplomacy, and governance have not changed much in our schools, universities and non- and informal systems of Education and learning (Wals et al., 2022). In this book, we ask the question what needs to be done for Education's role to materialise in an effective way. It recognises that our future depends on efforts to transform Education and learning so that it can challenge the way we engage with the natural environment and create alternative Just and Sustainable future.

Drawing on theoretical frameworks and practical experiences, the author will present a range of alternative approaches and non-reformist reforms to pave the way for more revolutionary changes in the larger society necessary for a more socially, just and environmentally Sustainable world. This will include climate/Sustainable /environmental Education, multicultural Education and critical pedagogy, Indigenous Education and knowledge, peace Education, and Education for social justice in relation to Teacher Education Curriculum as well as K-12 schools curriculum.

- The need to challenge dominant paradigms in Education and foster a more inclusive and equitable learning environment.

- The importance of incorporating diverse knowledge systems, including Indigenous knowledge, into Education.

- The potential of Education to promote social justice, environmental sustainability, and economic equity.

- The role of Education in empowering individuals and communities to challenge systemic inequalities and build a better future.

"We know that Education is critical to empower young people with the skills, knowledge and understanding needed to understand the root causes and consequences of Climate Change and prepare them to find solutions and to thrive in our changing world."

As the world faces a climate crisis, Education must be part of the answer." the author is using this space with a commitment to learning for the planet. These new voices sometimes push for approaches and paradigms that in the past have shown to be ineffective in our quest for a healthier planet. This highlights the importance of familiarising ourselves with the history and lessons learnt regarding the role of Education in learning to live within planetary boundaries. The author recognize the significance of engaging a broader group of stakeholders in the Educational process but also of the concern that a lack of context or learning can delay or side-track efforts to realise a better planetary future. It is for this reason that we seek to trigger a dialogue that enhances debates about the why, what, where and how of learning for the environment in the quest for more Just Sustainable futures. This Volume 1 book will be followed by a series of books in context of engaging other stakeholders in Education for Societal Transformation or better said ESD and ESG.

Education and learning are essential in helping citizens navigate their individual and collective efforts towards changing our systems and futures. In a sense, Education is the ultimate form of mitigation as it plays a key role in building democratic eco-literate societies underpinned with a desire for socio-ecological justice and an ethic of care. In the years to come, however, Education will need to be transformed to be able to take on this existential role at a rate faster than the pace of change we have seen over the last 50 years. Some might deem this too radical, but the current events affecting planet Earth are far more severe.

Contents

Chapter 1

Introduction

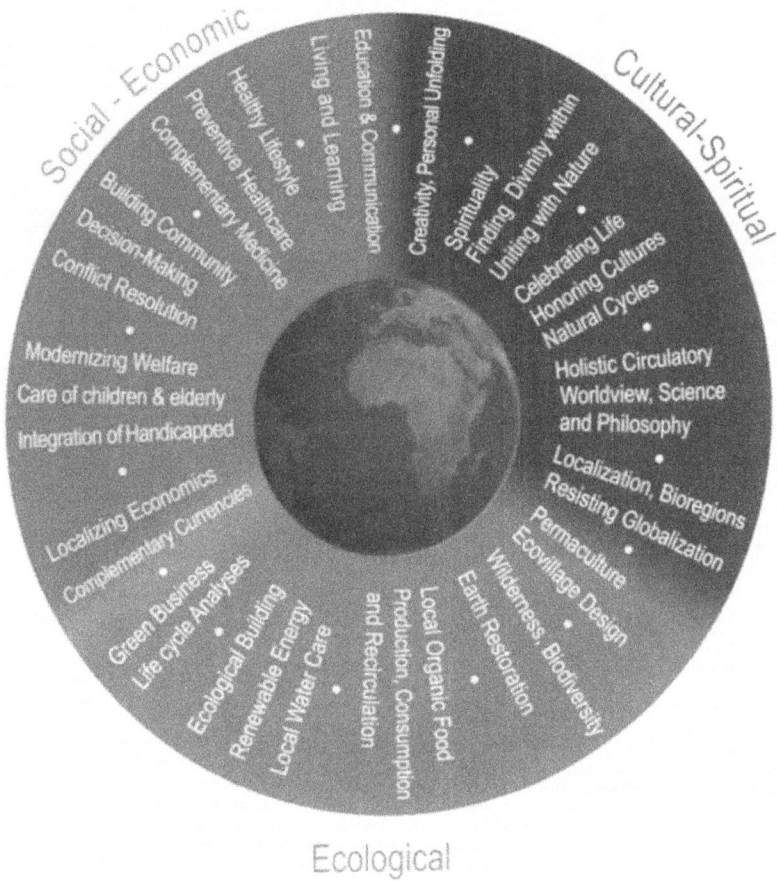

The importance of devoting urgent attention to Sustainable development is critical for the future of the planet and its people. According to scientists, Climate Change could threaten livelihoods, trigger conflicts, accelerate biodiversity loss, exacerbate disease outbreaks, destabilize political and social systems, cause economic shocks, and increase inequalities. The Sustainable Development Goals

(SDGs) are 17 ambitious objectives for a greener, healthier, more peaceful, and equal planet, agreed to by all governments, to be achieved by 2030.

Education for a Better World

To change course, the world needs many more of its citizens, especially the next generation, to have the knowledge, values, and skills to better navigate this uncertain future, tackle its profound challenges, and build more prosperous and resilient communities. Research shows that Education for Sustainable Development (ESD) is a crucial tool, which not only empowers students to shape a better world, but also perform better in school.

More than half of the population of our planet is currently under the age of 30 - the biggest generation of young people the world has ever seen. This puts educators in a truly unique position of influence to educate millions of students to overcome the greatest challenges of the 21st century and lead healthy and productive lives, in harmony with nature.

Education is a force that fosters agency, social mobility and innovation. But in the context of a changing climate, investing in Education is doubly important. Providing children with climate Education and green skills is critical to not only harnessing their power and aspirations, but also ensuring their adaptation to and preparation for the effects of Climate Change.

Yet the role of the Education systems in Climate Change National agendas has often been overlooked and not fully analyzed.

Research and Experimentation

Education 2030: A Gateway to Sustainable Development Goals

Rapid, sweeping, and long-lasting change is altering our planet's environment in an unprecedented manner, while societies are undergoing profound shifts in their demographic makeup and social and economic fabrics.

Political agreements, financial incentives or technological solutions alone do not suffice to grapple with the challenges of Sustainable development. It will require a wholesale change in the way we think and the way we act – a rethink of how we relate to one another and how we interact with the ecosystems that support our lives. To create a world that is more just, peaceful and Sustainable, all individuals and societies must be equipped and empowered by knowledge, skills and values as well as be instilled with a heightened awareness to drive such change.

This is where Education has a critical role to play. Education for Sustainable Development (ESD) is about shaping a better tomorrow for all – and this must start today.

The 17 Sustainable Development Goals (SDGs) are the world's best plan to build a better world for people and our planet by 2030. The SDGs are a call for action by all countries - poor, rich and middle-income - to promote prosperity while protecting the environment. They recognize that ending poverty must go hand-in-hand with strategies that build economic growth and address a range of social needs including Education, health, equality and job opportunities, while tackling Climate Change and working to preserve our ocean and forests.

There is growing International recognition of ESD as an integral element of quality Education and a key enabler for Sustainable development. Both the Muscat Agreement adopted at the Global Education for All Meeting (GEM) in 2014 and the proposal for Sustainable Development Goals (SDGs) developed by the Open Working Group of the UN General Assembly on SDGs (OWG) include ESD in the proposed targets for the post-2015 agenda. The proposed SDG 4 reads "Ensure inclusive and equitable quality Education and promote life-long learning opportunities for all".

The Education has to rise to the challenge of delivering the necessary skills for the future and move beyond the traditional subjects to include entrepreneurship, soft leadership, technology, and workforce readiness. And unless dramatic reforms in delivery, innovation, inclusion, and financing take place to change the trends in Education sector, the children may be left behind by the Global economy. They are likely to be unemployed, stuck in poverty, not contributing fully to their economies and societies, and dependent on government assistance. The opportunity to become drivers of or even participants in Industry 4.0 will remain just a dream. The world's already staggering income divide will widen and inequality will grow.

Objective:

The overall goal of this Proposal is to generate and scale up actions at all levels and areas of Education and learning to accelerate progress towards Sustainable development.

The National Government can use its reach create synergies for the required activities in member countries / various states, UT's and catalyse actions by other stakeholders. Government can play a key role in the following activities to ensure SDG integration into Education:

All of this serves our collective goal of preparing young people to address the urgent challenge of Climate Change.

Learning Goals

- Analyse curricular materials related to Climate Action (SD Goal #13) to frame and inform the curriculum for your learners.

- Explore "signature pedagogies" in Climate Change Education and learn how exemplary teachers design signature learning experiences for their students.

- Review research on effective approaches to Climate Change Education

- Understand the power of a school-wide strategy for climate action, addressing curriculum, teacher development and operations

- Receive feedback on your current challenges through the Think Tank's Consultancy—a protocol that facilitates reflection, peer coaching, and application of new ideas from the institute.

Transform Learning & Training Environment

Aim at helping Developing Member Countries (DMCs)/states develop sustainability plans in partnership with the broader community, and incorporate SDGs into its governance, administration and Education policy.

Unleashing a Systems Approach to Complex Development Challenges

SDG integration into Education will connect issues across sectors and thematic areas and leverage the creativity and knowhow of all – from National and local governments and communities to civil society, academia and the private sector – to build solutions that respond to people's daily challenges. This alone will promote contextual learning and help the states/DMCs/ reach their development ambitions.

Collaborate on Integrated Country Support Deliver an integrated and multidimensional approach to the SDGs by supporting DMCs deliver on their SDG ambitions, through integrated MAPS (Mainstreaming, Acceleration, and Policy Support) engagements, helping countries align on planning and budgeting processes to shift the goals from commitments to action.

Provide Operational/technical Services to states/UT's/ Business Entities

Offer its Technical Advisory services to states/UT's in human resources management, finance, procurement, ICT, and other administrative areas. This will enable Government and partners to operate effectively and cost-efficiently in complex operational contexts across the globe thereby synergistically linking investments, Partners/ Stakeholders and the SDG Goals.

Nextgen Policy and Programming

Solutions that worked well in the past are not adequate to address the challenges of today, and there is a need to disrupt our traditional approaches to development. Building on its network of experts, Government can help country to diagnose complex challenges to unlock a new generation of development solutions. These are solutions that connect Government with society, align planning and budgeting processes, and connect local and regional innovations and service delivery. NextGen policies and programmes can be creatively co-designed, for example through State Govt's/UT's Education departments that mobilise collective action for Sustainable development.

Suggested Framework

Ministry of Education Working Group 2030 project is recommended. The Sustainable Development Goals Division in the MOE, supported by a Nodal person in states/UT's, can spearhead it. The working group can.

- Collect ideas & examples of good practice for making the learning framework actionable.

- National, regional and local governments to share their policy design and curriculum design experiences related to the learning framework.

- Students, teachers, school leaders, and parents to share practices and experiences as concrete examples of using the SDG Learning Compass 2030 suggested by UN Global Compact organisation.

- Experts and researchers to help strengthen the links between evidence-based policy and practice, especially on the constructs of the framework.

- Local communities, professional associations and Education industry to share practices of supporting student learning and creating appropriate learning environments

- International communities and organisations to contribute to the "Education 2030" initiative.

Help partner countries co-create "design principles" for changes in curricula and Education systems that will be relevant for DMCs

The curriculum should be designed around SDG to motivate students recognise their prior knowledge, skills, attitudes and values.

The curriculum should be well-aligned with SDG goals, its teaching and assessment practices.

Topics should be based on real life projects on SDG, challenging students and enabling deep thinking and reflection.

While the technologies to assess many of the desired outcomes may not yet exist, different assessment practices might be needed for different purposes.

Higher priority be given to knowledge, skills, attitudes and values that can be learned in one context and transferred to others.

Process Design:

Teachers should be empowered to use their professional knowledge, skills and expertise to deliver the curriculum effectively based on SDG.

Learners should be able to link their learning experiences to the real world and have a sense of purpose in their learning.

Horizontal and Vertical integration of SDG will allow learners to discover how a topic or concept can link and connect to other topics or concepts within and across disciplines, and with real life outside of school.

The concept of "curriculum" should be developed from "predetermined and static" to "adaptable and dynamic". Schools and teachers should be able to update and align the curriculum to reflect evolving societal requirements as well as individual learning needs.

- Teachers, students and other relevant stakeholders should be involved early in the development of the curriculum, to ensure their ownership for implementation.

Design Appropriate Monitoring and Reporting Process

The mechanism for monitoring and reporting will also report on the implementation of National and International strategies to hold all relevant partners to account for their commitments as part of the overall SDG follow-up and review.

Recommendations

National Level

To better understand good practices and challenges, encourage voluntarily exchange of information on Education systems and policies across DMCs, more so in a region. Involve regional organizations to facilitate such exchanges

Global Level

Generate consensus Give countries chance to contribute to discussions on SDG 4 indicators in an informed and meaningful way.

Ensure decision-making mechanism of Technical Cooperation Group and strengthen its legitimacy

Foster Coordination

Introduce International household survey dedicated to Education Support monitoring of learning outcomes with code of conduct among donors to pool resources

Establish research hub related to the new Global indicators

We do not need a Technology-driven data revolution but rather

i. Better coordination between agencies

ii. More resources

Despite the formidable monitoring challenges related to the target, countries need to find ways to embed these themes in policies and curricula – including textbooks and other instruction Educational material s, joint research projects, community-based partnerships, projects with NGO's, International Development assistance projects, training and development assistance - in a way that impacts in achieving the sustainability goals and address local, National and Gobal challenges. Under ideal circumstances, SDG Target 4 requires preparing teachers to gain mastery over these themes, with ample resources for students to engage in individual and collaborative work, both inside and outside the classroom. Revamping current textbooks and Education materials with appropriate SDG learning elements can hasten the transformations required for Agenda 2030. We hope Education ministries and donors will take steps along this path.

The principle and scope of this emerging discipline on Sustainable development will be based on universal skills of effective thinking, acting, relating and accomplishing.

- Developing trialling and embedding creative and forward-looking SDG oriented cross cutting content in their National curriculum –

- Shared vision on SDG amongst institute s/ universities/ countries

- Collaboration amongst stakeholders

- Integrating SDG goals into the curriculum of Teacher Education (Pre/in service) and all Educational strategies (K-12) is the need of the hour.

- To aggressively pursue the SDG aspirations, we must empower/ elevate the stature of the teacher community to become SDG ambassadors and take this next evolutionary step of bringing SDG into Teacher Education curriculum. We need to exemplify the capacity and the value they hold on achieving this local/Global aspirations and lead the unprecedented transformation.

Clearly the status quo has to change. Can we imagine and create a state of the teacher profession as substantial authority on SDG in their organization and allow them to clearly demonstrate their qualification. We have to unite as a community of practice and help in integrating SDG practices into the teaching profession.

It is abundantly clear " You can't have a world class Education system without a world class Teacher Education system.

The ideology, ignorance and inertia on the part of the academia, experts, Aid agencies and policy maker, often explain why policies fail and why aid does not have the effect it should. A step-by-step approach towards a reimagined, reinvented, reengineered Education system is required that will not only effectively bring about quality Education and learning but will also help in fighting poverty and achieving other SDG goals.

MOE's strong commitment to International Education, research and collaboration can provide guidance to educators and ensure them an opportunity to become Global leaders of tomorrow, through implementing SDG goals, in a Sustainable manner.

Section I – Standards

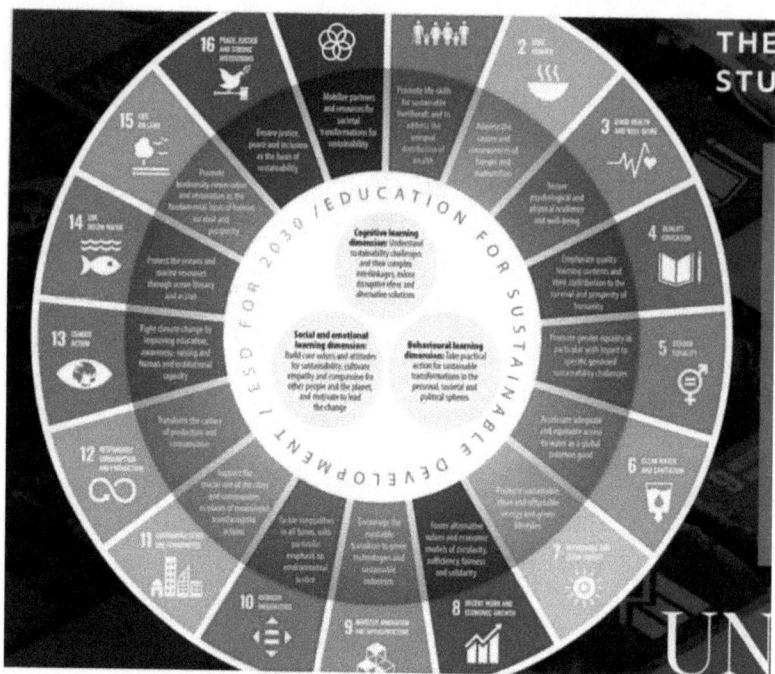

1. Direct engagement with young people. Youth are engaged and involved in efforts related to their future, especially closing the skills and employment gaps.

2. A focus on underserved youth. There is a commitment to identifying, monitoring, and targeting underserved youth with opportunities for skills and employment.

3. Inclusive and equitable, quality Education systems. Local Education systems are equitable, accessible, and sufficiently resourced. Local Education systems are equitable, accessible, and sufficiently resourced.

4. Pathways from Education to employment. Clear pathways exist in the city at the high school and post-secondary level.

5. Curriculum adapted to future workforce skills. Curriculum has explicit focus on 4IR skills (workforce readiness, soft skills, technical skills, entrepreneurship and resilience).

6. Employer engagement in building opportunity pipelines. Employers proactively engage with public policy officials, school systems and government agencies to build pathways from Education to employment.

7. Meaningful and equitable employment. Employment is meaningful, pays a livable wage and respects the dignity and contributions of young people.

8. Youth-focused funding partnerships. Local funding and philanthropy, from public to private, reflects the city's priority on youth futures through programs, subsidies, incentives, and scholarships.

9. Supportive ecosystem. The design of public services and policies create an ecosystem of support for young people on the pathway from Education to employment, including transportation, health care, mental health services, childcare and quality food.

10. Dedicated platform for opportunity dissemination and matchmaking.

Education and the SDGs

How Does Equitable and Quality Education Overlay and Intersect with Other SDGs

The SDGs acknowledge the importance of the interconnections between different issue areas and sectors that have traditionally been considered to be separate domains of expertise and practice. In response to this, inter Sectoral collaboration has come to be seen as a more efficient and effective way of working. This Book/Chapter aims to investigate and promote the interconnections between equitable and quality Education and other SDGs for holistic and systemic changes.

This chapter introduces the section on cross-Sectoral perspectives on Education, focusing on how Education can offer solutions and accelerate progress toward achieving the Sustainable Development Goals (SDGs). The world today faces new and complex challenges—ranging from Climate Change and technological upheavals to rising authoritarianism and Global inequities—that affect Education systems across the globe.

The Pivotal Role of Education

Education is often viewed as pivotal in creating and nurturing a more just, equitable and Sustainable world. It is clear that any move towards a more Sustainable future for our Global society and living world will require us to think of Education in its broadest sense - and not just about what is confined to a classroom or school-based system. This broad understanding of Education is important. If Education and learning are key to taking action on the climate and biodiversity crisis, then we need to consider multiple forms of Education and learning and what approach(es) are required for a Sustainable future.

Every conversation we have - for example with friends, family or colleagues - is a form of Education, and so the process of Education and learning is lifelong, universal and something that affects and connects us all. But we recognise that everyone has a different experience of teaching and learning. This is influenced by factors such as power dynamics, culture, and the value placed on various forms of knowledge.

Climate Change, environmental degradation, and climate shocks have an adverse impact on children's well-being and their ability to attend school and continue learning. These extreme weather events also affect schools and other teaching and learning infrastructure, in addition to affecting teachers and communities, potentially destroying entire

Education systems and putting a significant strain on countries' ability to provide Education.

How Policymakers Can Maximize Impact

The key to mitigating the impacts of climate disruption on Education is to get Education systems 'climate-ready'. As is the case with how we approach the climate crisis more broadly, preparation is better than cure.

Research shows that 55% of humanitarian funding is used for responding to crises that are predictable, with just 1% used for preparedness and early action. We need to flip this on its head.

Governments need to invest in 'preparedness', in building resilient Education systems with the processes, structures, depth of expertise and capacity to manage and adapt for sudden changes with minimum additional investment.

Resilient, prepared Education systems are capable of not just managing and mediating crises in the moment but are able to make decisions now to pre-empt future challenges.

Currently, approximately 1 billion children (i.e. nearly half of the world's children) live in countries that are at an extreme risk of suffering the impacts of Climate Change. The situation is further exacerbated in the East Asia and Pacific Region, where 41% of children face 5 or more overlapping climate and environmental shocks and stresses, as compared to a Global average of 14%.

We have to empower a generation of learners who can tackle the climate crisis.

The Covid Pandemic provided a powerful Global lesson in ecological literacy: everything is connected to everything. Within a period of months, a virus that evolved over hundreds of thousands of years among wild creatures spread like wildfire from one person to another to communities across every city on the planet, sickening tens of millions, shuttering business, and leaving hundreds of millions without work and income. People made tremendous sacrifices to protect their loved ones, co- workers, and communities. And a century of knowledge accumulation by evolutionary cell biologists, coupled with a vast interconnected Global economic infrastructure, culminated in vaccines that are now coursing through the veins of over a billion people. From species ecology, to human communities of commerce and care and science, to the ecology of the human body: Everything Connected.

This is the bewildering world that K-12 students must learn to comprehend. And to love. Why love? Because nature in its complexity provides the support systems for life. With eight headed to ten billion people on the planet, those support systems are massively threatened. If children do not gain ecological literacy—and the love of nature that flows from it—then there will be no political will to change the rules now causing ecological breakdown. Just as critically, there will be no business inspiration to change the game now leading us-- unchanged-- down a deeply unSustainable path. Environmental Education, sustainability Education, is the beating heart of the Theory of Change.

Given the increasing frequency of climate shocks, both adaptation and mitigation measures are critical to enable Education systems to adequately address Climate Change so that children continue to learn.

Equally, Education can be a powerful tool to mobilise climate action and lead the path to more Sustainable societies. The issue of Climate Change is being incorporated into various facets of Education policy and planning, post Covid 19 across countries.

Bringing together diverse and critical perspectives from policymakers, Education administrators, civil society, and multilateral organisations, in order to unpack the key issues and opportunities in mainstreaming the issue of Climate Change in Education systems.

The climate challenge is not just an environmental challenge, it is a human challenge. And Education plays a vital role in combating the climate crisis.

The new trends and perspectives spanning six key priorities through which action can be taken to reshape Educational planning are:

- How can digital technology help transform planning and management tools and approaches?

- How can Educational planning and management help address the learning crisis?

- How can planning and management better contribute to the promotion of gender equality in tomorrow's world?

- How can calls for transparency and new forms of funding enable planning to meet its objectives? • How planning can help Education systems adapt to crisis, Climate Change, and natural hazards?

- Developing skills for the future and the transition to work: How can planning help? These six priority areas reflect the more recent directions taken by UNESCO as reflected by IIEP's overall current research, training, and technical cooperation offer.

The main objectives are-

- To focus on the future of Education and how planners will be able to respond to the particular needs of society, today and tomorrow, in a context of rapid change, scarcity of resources, and increasing uncertainties;

- To explore the interconnected impact of political, geographical, and cross-Sectoral developments in Education and understand how Educational planning has been evolving and should continue to evolve to adapt to these changes;

- To bring together high-level decision makers, recognized International specialists, and IIEP's experts to stimulate new ideas on the best approaches, methods, tools and practices for Educational planning and management, with the goal of feeding them back into IIEP's research, training, and technical cooperation work;

- To revitalize and strengthen exchange and dialogue with an International community of thinkers and practitioners on Educational planning, with a view to better structuring and consolidating such a community in the future.

What Next?

Education can make an important contribution to sustainability but for it to truly deliver, major change is needed.

At a philosophical level, the magnitude of what faces humanity requires a more comprehensive eco-social framing of the sustainability challenge: one which encapsulates both Climate Change as a Global phenomenon and environmental issues as a more immediate and localized manifestation. We must concurrently address greenhouse gas emissions, the unsustainable use of resources and degrading of natural systems on which we rely.

Bringing the sustainability focus of Sustainable Development Goal target 4.7—to ensure all learners acquire knowledge and skills needed to promote Sustainable development by 2030—requires moving beyond knowledge to developing agency and empowering for action. Such a shift cannot be achieved by curriculum alone.

More attention is needed on pedagogical approaches and assessment that value, measure and incentivize agency as well as greater consideration of who are the 'agents' of change: teachers, students and parents.

The challenges are, however formidable. Foundational learning levels are abysmal and access to secondary Education, limited. Transformative Education is reliant on a well-prepared, supported and motivated teaching workforce which can't be assumed to always be in place.

All aspects of Education across research, learning, teaching and assessment can help tackle the climate crisis.

Education should be connected to other sectors and working in collaboration with them. New cross-sector partnerships will really drive forward climate action.

Educational Policies along six criteria has to be formulated –

1. Policy ambition. Does the country call for compulsory Education for Sustainable Development (ESD) or Climate Change Education (CCE) that is assessed with clear timebound benchmarks to monitor progress?

2. Pervasiveness. Does the country call for ESD/CCE across the Education system, including all levels of Education and across all subject areas?

3. Inclusiveness. Does the country's approach to ESD/CCE benefit all target populations, including the most vulnerable? Does the country engage and consult with educators and students during the ESD/CCE policymaking process?

4. Quality of Climate Change Education. Does the country call for ESD/CCE that is gender-empowering, intersectional, and transdisciplinary? Does it call for ESD/CCE that is based in science, fosters civic engagement and climate action, and builds pathways to future careers in the green economy?

5. Climate justice. Does the country center its approach to ESD/CCE in the pursuit of climate justice, by teaching how

different groups, like women and girls as well as indigenous peoples, are differentially impacted by Climate Change?

6. Systems strengthening. Does the country call for the adequate financing of public Education needed to support the delivery of quality ESD/CCE? Does the country ensure that teachers receive adequate training and continuing professional development to deliver quality ESD/CCE? There are glimmers of hope. Recent high-level publications from the FCDO, GPE, the World Bank and the Global Education Monitoring Team point to growing awareness of the challenge and need for rigor in climate- Education research—something also evident in the climate, environment and Education group currently co-chaired by FCDO and GPE.

7. As to immediate practical challenges, there's growing attention being paid to anticipatory action and infrastructure. And finally, the emphasis of the 2025 PISA science assessment conducted by OECD on essential competencies for 'agency in the Anthropocene' suggests that in some minds, an action-orientated paradigm shift has already begun. There is hope for the future, but it stems not just from knowing but also doing. Education that empowers is the key.

Section II – The Climate Crisis is a Child Rights Crisis

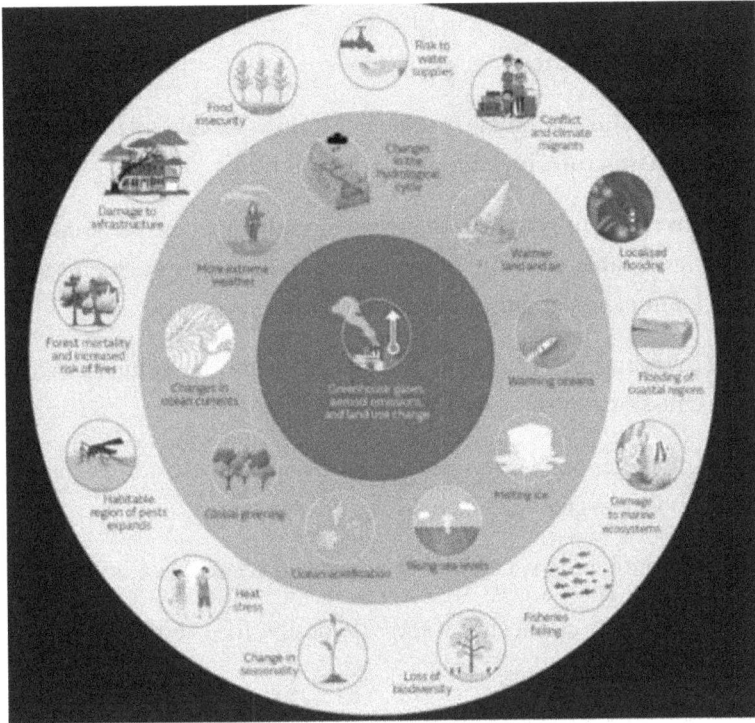

Failing to protect children from climate and ecological crises is a violation of their rights. Safeguarding these rights today and into the future means both recognizing which hazards children face and understanding their impact.

The Child Right Crisis principle of the right to life, survival and health can guide decisionmakers to invest in climate- resilient infrastructure for schools and homes; green technology; climate Education; and policy reform to phase out fossil fuels. Children's unique vulnerabilities and needs must be reflected in all action on the climate crisis.

The principles of the CRC spotlight where we must focus policies and plans so that children inherit a habitable planet, enjoy a minimum standard of living and benefit from a more equal society and peaceful world.

We must take a future-focused approach to realizing child rights by Expanding climate resilience through

- Integrating climate resilience into local planning and infrastructure, including schools and health centers.

- Investing in climate Education to equip children for building a Sustainable future. • Ensuring children's needs are addressed in National Adaptation Plans and climate strategies.

- Investing in renewable energy and promote solutions to cut emissions by 43% by 2030.

- Implementing large-scale ecosystem restoration and Sustainable land management practices.

- Strengthening waste management and combat pollution.

- Delivering connectivity and safe design for every child

There are no Human Rights on a Dead Planet

Two decades after the Earth Summit, the importance of effectively engaging these nine sectors of society was reaffirmed by the United Nations Conference on Sustainable Development (UNCSD), also known as the Rio+20 Conference. Its outcome document "The Future We Want" highlights the role that Major Groups can play in pursuing sustainable societies for future generations. The "Major Groups" include:

WOMEN · CHILDREN AND YOUTH · INDIGENOUS PEOPLE · LOCAL COMMUNITIES · EDUCATIONAL & ACADEMIC ENTITIES · FAITH GROUPS

I-GOVERNMENTAL ORGANIZATIONS · LOCAL AUTHORITIES · WORKERS & TRADE UNIONS · FOUNDATIONS & PRIVATE PHILANTHROPIC ORGANISATIONS · MIGRANTS & THEIR FAMILIES · OLDER PERSONS

BUSINESS & INDUSTRY · SCIENTIFIC & TECHNOLOGICAL COMMUNITY · FARMERS · PARLIAMENTARY NETWORKS & ASSOCIATIONS · PERSONS WITH DISABILITIES · VOLUNTEER GROUPS

Championing Education Change: Human Rights and the Climate Crisis

More than Four years into the COVID-19 pandemic, we are witnessing a colossal loss to children's learning. Less than half of countries are implementing learning recovery strategies at scale to help children catch up. Unless all countries implement and expand programs in the coming months, they risk losing a generation.

"With a combined 2 trillion hours of in-person school lost due to school closures since March 2020, students in more than 4 in 5 countries fell behind in their learning. Less well-off children have seen their learning falling back. In particular, the most marginalised – those living in poverty and rural areas, children with disabilities, and the youngest students – have fallen the furthest behind.

"Basic, foundational skills upon which every aspect of Education is built have been erased in many countries. Children have forgotten how to read and write; some are unable to recognise letters. Children who were poised to start school for the first time never got the chance to learn these skills in the first place, as early childhood Education disappeared in most countries. Without urgent remedial action, this could carry serious lifelong consequences in terms of health and well-being, future learning and employment.

World Bank Press Release in 2022 on Education Crisis across countries - data shows that less than half of countries featured in a new analysis published are implementing learning recovery strategies at scale to help children catch up on what they've missed. Only half of low-income countries have a plan in place to assess where those who have returned are at in their learning.

"At a time when it's needed the most, Education funding has and continues to fall desperately short. Countries allocated on average 3 per cent of their COVID-19 stimulus packages to Education. In low- and lower-middle-income countries, the allocation was less than 1 per cent.

"While countries scramble to recover, they are overlooking the single, most-effective long-term recovery and sustainability tool – Education.

"Governments must double down efforts get every child into school. Education is a fundamental human right. The multiple and intersecting barriers – including poverty, cultural norms, and poor quality teaching – preventing children from accessing their Education must be broken down. Every child needs to be assessed on their learning and based on the results, they must have access to quality, tailored, catch-up classes to recover what they've lost and beyond. Teaching should be adjusted to the level they currently are at in their learning. Teachers must be given the training, support and resources they need. And finally, schools must go beyond places of learning and support children's well-being and safety.

"This is a now-or-never moment to act and transform Education in order to save this generation and the only way out is through Climate Change Education.

Climate Change is a human rights issue, and how human rights can be used as a tool to combat the climate crisis. Global warming violates key human rights, yet human rights can be used as an effective tool to counteract the effects and continued growth of Global warming.

Choosing Our Future: Education for Climate Action-

The UNESCO Committee on The Right to Child has reported the urgent need to address the adverse effects of environmental degradation, with a special focus on Climate Change, on the enjoyment of children's rights, and clarifies the obligations of States to address environmental harm and Climate Change. The Committee also explains how children's rights under the Convention on the Rights of the Child apply to environmental protection, and confirms that children have a right to a clean, healthy and Sustainable environment.

Education systems can empower, equip, and skill young people for climate mitigation and adaptation. At the same time, Climate Change induced heat and extreme weather events are significantly disrupting learning, and low-income countries are disproportionately affected. Governments must act now to adapt Education systems for Climate Change.

Experts reveal science-based blueprint for rebuilding Education systems. The recent International Science and Evidence based Education Assessment report by UNESCO MGIEP identifies a key driver to the growing inequity that spills over to the stratification of societal structures into the "haves"' and "have nots". Professor Dr. Anantha Duraiappah, the Director of UNESCO' s Mahatma Gandhi Institute of Education for Peace and Sustainable Development, shares how the Education sector has failed the promises of the Universal Declaration of Human Rights.

In a historical achievement for humankind almost 75 years ago, the Universal Declaration of Human Rights clearly recognized Education as a basic human right. Although a non-legally binding document, it became the first International instrument to acknowledge the importance of Education for individuals and societies. Today we find Education a booming industry with privatization having taken hold of the sector. This commodification of Education has inevitably created an elitist system of private schools with the best funded providing the "best" Education to those who can afford the fees for attending these private schools. This forms what Daniel Mokovit's Markovits in his book "'The Meritocracy Trap" a new aristocracy in the form of heritage meritocracy.

As we look to 2050, we face a choice. We can continue on our current path, risking a future where millions of children are left behind, or we can choose a different course – one where every child flourishes and shapes the world around them. Now is the time to shape a better future for every child.

Chapter 2

Introduction to the UN SDG's or the Global Goals

SDGs as Global Governance of Education - Integrate governance and Sustainability to create a Sustainable future

Ten years into the 17 Sustainable Development Goals (SDGs), the SDGs have increasingly been embedded into National discourse and planning, as well as our everyday activity. They have been adopted as the standards for government success across countries.

Given the influence Global goals can have, Education sector can set out to explore how the SDGs have been shaped and further shape the activities and plans of nation-states. Global governance is increasingly recognised in the Education space, as governance extends beyond the nation-states and an increased number of intergovernmental organisations, civil society and private sector actors work collectively toward a Global common interest.

17 goals and five years left until the world reaches the deadline for the Sustainable Development Goals for the people, planet and prosperity. With the clock ticking, Education must be prioritized to accelerate progress toward all the SDGs, especially amid growing inequalities and fast-evolving challenges.

The world needs to invest in Education because this is the only path toward Sustainable development. All other priorities for development – the economy, healthcare, livelihoods, Climate Change action, etc. – depend on human resources. The world needs people who are educated to do new jobs, do them well, and with the necessary skills.

There is no development without Education, and Education is the greatest force to reduce inequality.

Education and investment in future generations can provide a useful and impactful approach for companies and investors to promote progress, achieve better financial outcomes, and improve ESG performance. There is growing evidence that Education is material for businesses and investors. However, a paradigm shift is needed in order to link Education and ESG more effectively, and the further development of a framework is an important first step.

To achieve these outcomes, this book can be a vehicle for driving more active engagement and investment in Education programs and policies, unlocking broader ESD/CCE benefits, advancing sustainability objectives.

Learn for Our Planet, Act for the Climate

Our Commitment

1. We recognise Education as a society-wide learning process that can equip everyone with knowledge, skills, values and attitudes needed for urgent action to combat Climate Change.

2. We commit to the integration of sustainability and Climate Change in formal Education systems, including as core curriculum components, in guidelines, teacher training, examination standards and at multiple levels through institutions.

3. We similarly commit to the integration of sustainability and Climate Change in professional training, public awareness and information activities, and other areas of non-formal and informal learning. We consider it crucial to support out of school activities geared towards sustainability.

4. We commit to enhancing multi-stakeholder and cross-Sectoral collaboration with strong partnership between our Education and environment sectors.

5. We commit to working with and support the private sector to meet its responsibilities for green and carbon-neutral economies, which requires a workforce attuned to sustainability.

6. We commit to working with diverse stakeholders, including young people, to ensure proposed policies and changes adequately respond to the needs and lived experiences of all communities.

7. We commit to highlighting Education and learning within adaptation efforts including National adaption plans (NAPs) and Disaster Risk Reduction (DRR) measures, and to increase our efforts to ensure that our Education systems are resilient in the face of Climate Change.

8. We commit to taking the provisions of this declaration forward, including, as appropriate, through specific pledges within our respective mandates and in our areas of responsibility, taking into account our needs, capacities, available resources and National priorities, and as we continue our urgent work to meet the provisions of the Paris Agreement. We agree to review our joint commitment in advance of COP27.

9. Investment in Education has the power and ability to both improve society and drive business results. Investment in Education, human development, and training is an investment in today and future generations. Positioning Education at the core is a useful and impactful way to advance the objectives of companies and investors seeking to achieve better financial outcomes and improve Environmental, Social, and Governance (ESG) performance and credibility.

10. Share information about youth-development programs which will grant students the opportunity to organize Climate Teach-ins in their institution, gain professional experience in sustainability Education, earn a Certificate in Climate Organizing, and connect with a growing network of climate activists, educators and professionals.

11. Empowers individuals and groups to organize for progressive causes. We encourage responsible activism, and do not support using the platform to take unlawful or other improper action. We do not control or endorse the conduct of users and make no representations of any kind about them.

12. Making Policy Actionable: Learn how to influence decision-making and integrate climate Education into meaningful policies. Tools to shape meaningful policy outcomes.

13. Crafting Powerful Narratives: Build stories that inspire action and resonate with the stakeholders who matter.

14. Collaborate on actionable strategies in the Policy Strategy Roundtable.

15. Analyse real-world successes with Case Studies to uncover what works.

16. Engage directly with climate leaders in an Open Forum & Panel Discussion.

Let's Make Climate Education the Cornerstone of Climate Action!

SDGs as Product & Mechanism

The SDGs are a product of the diverse, multi-stakeholder space of Global governance. The array of actors from different political, economic, and cultural backgrounds proposed a wide-ranging set of goals. The SDGs were the product of this contested negotiation between actors with background documents in the run up to the SDGs reflecting differences in ideologies and views of Education quality and inclusion.

Despite its shortcomings, the creation of the SDGs did more to increase the voice of nation-states, civil society, and other sectors of society than prior goal creation. Soft governance was better able to accommodate the varied interests present and foster consensus, than sanction-based hard governance approaches. The end product was the broad and ambitious overarching goal of SDG 4, "Ensure inclusive and equitable quality Education and promote lifelong learning opportunities for all".

While the SDGs can be viewed as a product of actors working to influence the SDGs to meet their needs, the SDGs can also be understood as a mechanism, independently influencing the discourse and activity of nation-states. This is done through three governance channels: governing through goals, governing through numbers, and governing through morality.

The challenges of governance for Sustainable development in a globalizing world are real and many. National governments must coordinate policy development and implementation with diverse actors — businesses, local governments, regional/International institutions, and civil society organizations. The Global Information and communication revolution is leading to increased transparency, with growing demands for participation in decision making in every country.

The world urgently needs a practical and effective framework for Sustainable development to address the simultaneous challenges of ending poverty, increasing social inclusion, and sustaining local and planetary life systems.

Gain Knowledge of the UN SDGs to Help Make a Positive Impact

It is unequivocal that human actions are causing widespread environmental damage. To help combat this, the UN Sustainable Development Goals (SDGs) provide a blueprint to address environmental challenges and achieve a brighter future for both people and the planet.

Sustainable human rights and society, Sustainable economy, and Sustainable environment to help you systematically explore the SDGs.

Taking into account the adverse impacts of Climate Change on human health, the importance of increasing knowledge and gaining essential skills is necessary to mitigate and adapt to its impacts and protect human health. Researchers and experts are urging for more research in the climate-health nexus, as well as calling for efforts that establish climate and health Educational goals. They encourage the development of agreed upon, articulated science-based curricula and resources addressing climate-health issues. This review aims to map out the current state of integration of Climate Change Education in school-based Education across the world and identify the human health topics included. Furthermore, to explore the extents to which levels of prevention and health co-benefits of climate mitigation and adaptation are covered within the framework of school-based Climate Change Education.

Explore Human Rights and the Sustainable Economy

Different SDGs that relate to human rights and a Sustainable economy. This includes Sustainable cities and communities (SDG 11), decent work and economic growth (SDG 8), and affordable and clean energy (SDG 7).

Unpack the SDGs from the perspective of a Sustainable Environment

Uncover the ways SDGs can contribute to a Sustainable environment. Delving into climate action (SDG 13), life below water (SDG 14), life on land (SDG 15), and more, you'll gain insights into how to protect our planet effectively. Climate crisis is changing the world we live in. Climate experts all point to these extremes as clear signs that action must be taken to ensure a Sustainable future – but what does action really look like?

- Develop background knowledge of the 17 Sustainable Development Goals (SDGs)

- Explore the connection of SDGs and human rights, economy, and the environment

- Develop the ability to analyze the National and foreign policy on the SDGs-related agenda

- Engage in shaping our common future and contributing to the betterment of society as a Global citizen

- Explore more interdisciplinary talks and discussion on the SDGs issues • Empowering sustainability through data, analysis and Global best practice

- Demonstrating a commitment to sustainability and positive social impact is essential, but providing evidence of that commitment is not always easy. Data experts will demonstrate how our unique data can help deliver on the SDGs. Through masterclasses, talks, case studies and 1:1 demos, DataLabs can show higher Education institutions, governments and businesses how to forge strategic partnerships and optimise their sustainability strategies.

- Feasible pathways to long-term sustainability are highly complex, subject to technological uncertainty, and requiring substantial financial resources. Sound policy-making in each country requires a long-term approach that integrates strategies vis-à-vis many challenges: food and nutritional security, social service delivery, energy policy, water resource management, urbanization, infrastructure, human rights, biodiversity, adaption to Climate Change, mitigating GHGs, Sustainable business, good governance, and much more.

- New kinds of cross- disciplinary expert teams, knowledgeable of and sensitive to these issues, and often working across National borders, are needed to provide an integrated approach to sustainability.

Section I - The Role of Higher Education in Addressing Environmental Challenges

Planning is the Starting Point for Climate-Resilient Education Systems

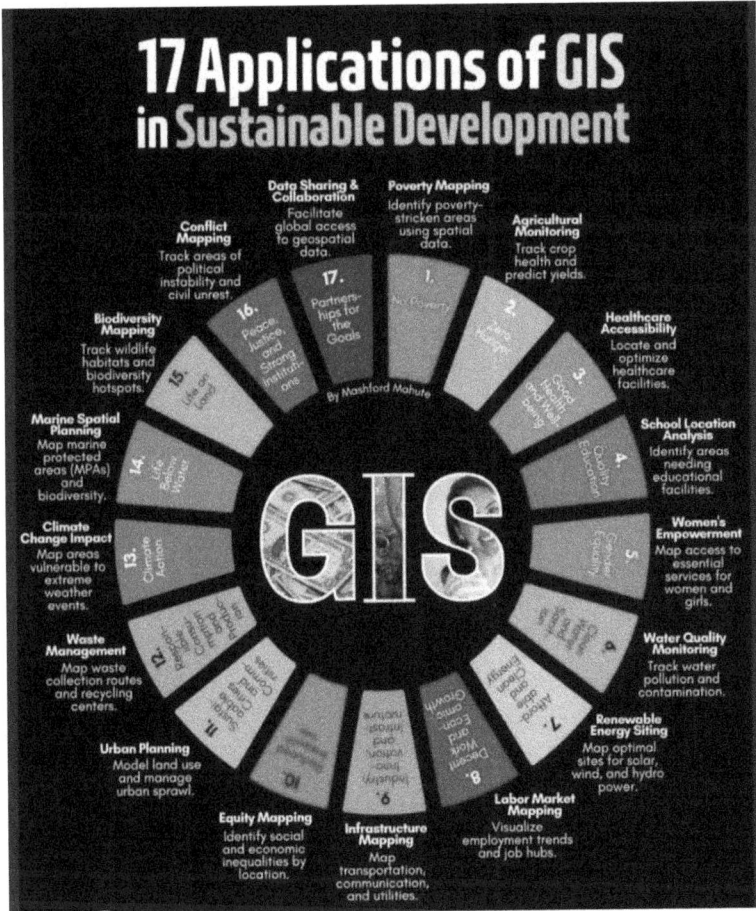

Education is increasingly vulnerable to Climate Change, but has an important role to play in helping learning communities and Education systems mitigate and adapt to it.

Educational planning that is sensitive to Climate Change, is the starting point for climate-resilient Education systems and an opportunity for a different future.

In this sense, Education is not just a victim of Climate Change. It is part of the solution and can accelerate climate action. But Education actors must fully understand risks and know where and when to integrate various adaptation and mitigation measures into the Educational planning cycle.

Making all Stages of the Planning Cycle Climate-Resilient

No matter where a country is in the planning cycle, relevant and effective measures can be put in place. This is especially true when planning represents the voices of many – e.g., National and sub-National authorities, school communities, and youth, including the most vulnerable, such as girls or young women.

Mitigation and adaptation measures should ideally be mainstreamed from the start of the planning cycle, either as an integral part of an Education sector analysis (ESA) or as an Education sector risk assessment.

Crisis-sensitive planning aims to mainstream Climate Change to ensure that all Education actors – including communities, students, teachers, and middle-tier leaders– can anticipate, prepare for, and adapt to the effects of Climate Change. At the central level, this includes creating a conducive policy framework, as well as fostering Education for Sustainable development (ESD) through the inclusion of Climate Change in curricula and teacher training. At the middle-tier and school levels, this includes school-level contingency plans with a focus on localized climate-change threats, and the construction of climate-resilient school infrastructure.

But a Plan is Only as Good as its Implementation

To ensure effective implementation of climate-related measures, ministries of Education and their partners need to involve subnational authorities, local communities, and youth, including those most impacted by Climate Change. These should then be underpinned by monitoring plans and accompanied by evidence- based costing and financing models.

Together, Education stakeholders should conduct regular monitoring to track progress on Climate Change measures and reorient strategies considering new developments and information.

To this end, strengthening Education management information systems (EMIS) to collect and analyze Climate Change data requires consultation with stakeholders from multiple sectors, including from ministries of environment and National disaster management authorities.

Around the world, college and university students have become increasingly concerned and vocal about climate action. This is a powerful and growing movement that has the potential to change the course of history, yet it is unclear that climate demonstrations or divestment protests will have the desired outcome of comprehensive systemic change to avoid climate disaster.

What is recommended is that students/activists, Policy makers, all stakeholders including academia civil society, NGOs - should together share ideas, learn, connect, and act on the Global imperative of addressing Climate Change. Offered in the context of the Global climate negotiations, this program challenges student teams around the world to propose ideas for local-scale projects that will yield measurable results over a stipulated time. Accepted teams become a cohort that learns together, networks, shares ideas, and contribute to a growing body of inspirational projects that demonstrate the capacity of today's youth to lead and have an impact.

All proposals must be actionable by students without extensive contingencies and should be designed to yield measurable results over the course of six months. Proposals may reflect ongoing projects and activities so long as they are the intellectual capital of the students applying and there is a projected measurable outcome during the duration of the Forum implementation period. Students will be required to attend online workshops and encouraged to interact with each other over the six months of the Forum. Final projects will be collected into an online publication and showcased in an event after the 2023 climate COP in Abu Dhabi.

The Environmental Innovations Initiative at the University of Pennsylvania leads the Global University Climate Forum on behalf of the International Sustainable Campus Network as a way to engage and inspire the next generation of climate leaders and showcase the value of academic institutions as the Knowledge Sector.

United Nations Framework Convention on Climate Change, in addition to showcasing the activities and remarkable contributions of the students of the Global University Climate Forum, this important publication showcases how we can and should rely on universities to teach and research while elevating the thought leadership of today's college and university students.

Conducts research on the psychological, cultural, and political factors that influence environmental attitudes and behavior; teaches students; informs and engages the public through environmental journalism; and supports a Global network of organizations seeking to build public and political will for environmental solutions.

Show how schools, leaders, and communities are making an impact in mitigating Climate Change, creating collaborative learning opportunities, and advancing equity in community approaches.

What does the Education sector need to do in order to respond to the challenges of Climate Change? Educators and leaders are already driving impact in their schools and communities — embracing evidence-based solutions, innovative practices, and an emerging consensus around Education as a key lever for climate action. How can we broaden that vision and scale that impact? These questions and more were explored at a Harvard Graduate School of Education convening on Education and Climate Action, a half-day event that welcomed Education and policy leaders from around the country to the Askwith Hall stage to grapple with the most pressing issues at the intersection of Education and climate — and look toward meaningful solutions.

"Climate Change is not a future problem; Climate Change is already happening, and it affects us all," said Dean Bridget Long, kicking off the event. But the most serious consequences of climate disruption are not being felt equally, she said. "Climate Change is exacerbating Educational inequality. It is now another important cause of the inequities that so many of us are working hard to address. So, we need to take action and with about 70 million students enrolled in school from PreK through postsecondary Education, one in five Americans are currently connected to the Education sector, making Education a critical lever for change. What we do matters."

The time is now for us to do this. The impacts are here today. Students, families, and communities are feeling them across the country and the world, and that is only going to increase. So, the time is now.

When it comes to Climate Change, young people around the globe have employed both leadership and passion to propose and demand solutions from the adults in charge. Yet with the support of educators, we can empower these young people to be even more engaged and effective in this work. What can we do to better equip our students with the knowledge to deeply understand Climate Change, so they can help to develop climate solutions? How can we embed Climate Change across subjects and disciplines to foster deep knowledge of the topic among young people? How can we help our youth become better communicators — and better advocates for climate action?

Section II - Taking Action through Education and Learning

Action through Education and learning can take many forms - and connects and affects us all. Truly meaningful and effective climate action requires engagement with, and contributions from, all stakeholders.

Here, we highlight action projects across the world and the ways in which they engage diverse communities.

Why Climate Change Education for Social Transformation?

With a joint systems thinking on climate crisis and the role of Climate Change Education for social transformation. This volume will explore the gaps in Education policies and curriculum, and where we want to go in view of the needed social transformation towards decarbonisation and sustainability as well as the renewed understanding of Climate Change Education today.

Action for Climate Empowerment (ACE) is a term adopted by the UN Framework Convention on Climate Change (UNFCCC) to denote work under Article 6 of the Convention and Article 12 of the Paris Agreement. The overarching goal of ACE is to enable all members of society to engage in climate action through the six ACE elements:

1. Climate Change Education
2. Public awareness
3. Training
4. Public participation
5. Public access to information
6. International cooperation on these issues.

UNESCO Green Citizens supports and highlights local citizen-led projects that are shaping new ways of inhabiting the world, in harmony with nature.

UNESCO Green Citizens is a valuable resource. In the words of a Participant at COP29 - "Give me sustainability of substance, not of words - no matter how beautiful they are - not of commitments that have no backing, that are just 'politics'.

We can't play politics with life. We can't play politics with these issues. Give me sustainability of substance and I will give you the future."

Regional Centres of expertise (RCEs) in Education for Sustainable Development It is vital that there is meaningful representation from marginalised and indigenous communities at key Global events such as COP's to ensure that the aims of ACE are fulfilled to support community action on Climate Change.

Youth, Children and Education at COP29

When we aim to make the world a better place, we must consider the largest section of society – the youth. In these modern times, where globalization is ever- transcending and technology is a part of our everyday lives – the youth is connected with the world more than ever. Today's youth have the opportunity to interact with and learn from powerful people and organizations over the internet. The United Nations (UN) has acknowledged the significant role of youth in advancing the Sustainable Development Goals. As active citizens of the world, the youth care for the environment, social responsibility, diversity, and inclusion, and fearlessly voice their opinions on social media and call for action. Youth activists like Greta Thunberg and Alexandria Villasenor shook the world expressing their concerns, mobilizing people, and demanding action and attention from leaders worldwide. Organizations such as the UNICEF promote youth involvement by calling for young leaders to participate in annual summits on Global issues. Therefore, youth voices are being heard and reflected upon, on a Global scale and must continue being heard to progress towards a responsible world. Sustainability and Sustainable development are critical issues today that impact any and every section of the society.

Therefore, empowering students to discuss and brainstorm solutions to such Global issues will increase awareness of the gravity of the situation and create an urgency for immediate action. Students have an influential position to lead a change movement within their respective communities as well as across countries. When students across the world join hands to advance the values of sustainability, we can witness a future of responsible citizens proactively managing Global issues, taking purposeful action, and fearlessly working towards a peaceful and Sustainable world. The 2020 World Youth Report also highlights the role of young people in the realm of Sustainable development, particularly related to the implementation of 2030 Agenda for Sustainable Development. The report refers to youth as the 'torchbearers' of 2030 agenda and shares insights on their role in working with the local and National government and delivering policies and programmes on the ground.

The future of inclusive responsible management Education relies heavily on students. They are considered the most important stakeholders. The future will be made by students leading the sustainability space.

COP28, in Dubai, provided a new spotlight on Education; creating the first Youth, children, Education and skills day ever held at a COP.

This catalysed 37 countries to sign the Declaration on the common agenda for Education and Climate Change which foregrounded the crucial link between Education and climate action as key to a safe, resilient future for all. This declaration was the first global, political acknowledgement of the importance of Education; particularly for those young people impacted, displaced and disproportionately affected by Climate Change.

This emphasis was maintained and progressed at COP29.Following an agreement at COP29, there is now an appointed Presidency Youth Climate Champion for COP30; aiming to 'enhance and encourage the inclusive engagement of children and young people in climate decision-making and policy processes by utilising the unique position of each COP Presidency'.

The COP29 Presidential action agenda – includes a Human Development Day, taking 'a holistic view of Climate Change that treats human development, youth, health and Education as inter-related issues to be supported, while also addressing each thematic issue as a stand-alone priority'.

Empowerment through Climate Literacy

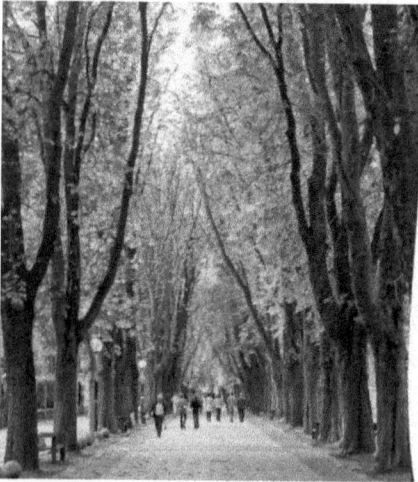

Five Key Characteristics

Collaborative, Welcoming, and Responsive Learning Environment

Knowledge and Skills for Climate Action

Attention on Climate Emotions

Locally Focused and Community Driven

Civic Engagement for Climate Action

We live in an era of poly-crises and are in need of transitions toward a more Sustainable world. There are no blueprints for this immense endeavour; instead, we must explore and learn our way out of unsustainable living. Education for Sustainable Development (ESD) can help us with the knowledge, tools and means for that.

"We stand upon the shoulders of great educators and organisations who 'walked the talk' by bringing the head, heart and hands into meaningful change towards the future."- Steering committee Dutch ESD Program.

"Elevated knowledge and awareness as to the scale and urgency of ecological crisis that is upon us is only one aspect of what is needed in changing our impact. Understanding what has been achieved and what more needs to be done is an essential starting point. Without nature, there is no future; without Education, there is no understanding.

A valuable insight into how Education can play a pivotal role in shaping a more Sustainable world amidst the challenges of Climate Change and other environmental shifts is the need of the hour.

The urgency of addressing Climate Change and environmental degradation has never been greater. The consequences for children's health and well-being and for the stability and resilience of their communities are profound.

An educated and skilled young generation is humanity's most powerful tool to combat the interconnected Global challenges we face, including poverty, inequality, Climate Change and fragility.

A Three-Step Climate Risk Analysis to Build Education System Resilience

3 steps to help Education planners and policy makers better understand the threats posed by Climate Change and prepare to withstand and adapt to them.

The program is designed to help countries integrate Climate Change adaptation and environmental sustainability into Education sector plans, budgets and strategies.

Producing a climate risk analysis is key to shape and inform broader Education planning efforts.

Education can be a powerful driver for more Sustainable development, including a transition to green societies.

How Does One Go About Conducting a Climate Risk Analysis for the Education Sector?

To guide planners and policy makers, IIEP has developed a three-step methodology for climate risk analyses in the Education sector. This involves analyzing the effects of climate risks and identifying the existing strengths and weaknesses of the Education system at the institutional, organizational and individual levels.

Step 1: Identifying and analyzing key climate stressors A climate-risk analysis begins with an examination of a country's main climate stressors by analyzing historical climate trends and future projections. This first step focuses on understanding the specific nature and frequency of each stressor, such as heat waves, drought, floods and cyclones, and how they are likely to evolve in the context of Climate Change. By grounding the analysis in historical and projected climate data, planners gain a clear understanding of the specific risks facing the Education sector now and in the future.

Step 2: Understanding the effects of Climate Change on Education After mapping the main climate stressors, the next step is understanding the exposures and vulnerability of schools and the Education system to climate risks and analyzing the impact on Education at both National and subnational levels. Climate Change disrupts Education in various ways, from limiting access to harming learning quality and upending Education system management processes like school supervision and data collection. At this stage, the risk analysis draws on a broad range of Education data and information to explore four key areas: access to Education, learning quality, system management, and equity in Education. Triangulating climate and Education data also enables planners to quantify the impact of Climate Change on the Education system.

Step 3: Analysing capacities for climate resilience Identifying risks and their impacts on Education is only the beginning. It is equally crucial to assess the resources and capacities available to manage them. Building resilience requires that countries bolster the ability of Education stakeholders—from ministries to school leaders and students—to respond effectively to climate challenges.

This third step examines current capacities and identifies capacity gaps within the Education system – from the individual through to the institutional level- to mitigate the effects of Climate Change.

Towards a Climate-Resilient Future for Education

Through this three-step climate risk analysis, Education planners can better understand the threats posed by Climate Change and, more importantly, prepare to withstand and adapt to them.

By identifying climate stressors, assessing the effects of climate risks, and analyzing capacities, countries can subsequently develop effective strategies, plans and policies to safeguard Education.

7 things to keep in mind when trying to engage youth in a meaningful way that drives outcomes –

1. Recognize and Value Youth Voices: Acknowledge the importance of including youth perspectives in Global events and discussions. Understand that their unique insights, creativity, and commitment can lead to meaningful change.

2. Connect Global and Local Contexts: Encourage discussions and initiatives that bridge the Global with the local. Find common ground where Global issues align with regional concerns, allowing youth to relate their experiences and expertise to broader challenges.

3. Empower Action: Facilitate opportunities for youth to translate knowledge into action. Inspire them to take tangible steps

toward positive change, such as organizing local initiatives or projects based on the insights gained from Global events.

4. Foster Inclusivity: Promote an inclusive environment where youth are active participants in meaningful discussions rather than passive observers. Ensure their voices are heard, valued, and integrated into the broader dialogue.

5. Collaborate Across Generations: Encourage intergenerational collaboration. Allow youth forums to intersect with main panels, creating opportunities for cross-generational discussions, knowledge sharing, and mentorship.

6. Amplify the Impact of Youth Voices: Recognize that collective action is more powerful. Encourage collaboration among youth, enabling them to work together to drive change on a larger scale.

7. Continuously Optimize Youth Engagement: Regularly assess and refine strategies for engaging youth effectively. Seek feedback from young participants and stakeholders to adapt and improve the engagement process for better outcomes.

Principles of Responsible Management of Education

Principle

1. Principle 1 - Develop the abilities of students to be future generators of Sustainable value for business and society in general and to work for an inclusive society and Sustainable Global economy.

2. Principle 2 Values- Incorporate into academic activities and study programs the values of social responsibility worldwide as described in International initiatives such as the United Nations Global Compact.

3. Principle 3 Method - Create Educational frameworks, materials, processes and environments that allow effective learning experiences for responsible leadership.

4. Principle 4 Research - Commit to a conceptual and empirical research that increases our knowledge about the role, dynamics and impact of corporations in the creation of Sustainable social, environmental and economic value.

5. Principle 5 Collaboration - Interact with the managers of corporate corporations to expand our knowledge of their challenges in fulfilling social and environmental responsibilities and to jointly explore effective ways to address these challenges.

6. Principle 6 - Facilitate and support dialogue and debate among educators, students, businesses, government, consumers, the media, civil society organizations and other interested groups and stakeholders on critical issues related to Global social responsibility and sustainability.

7. Principle 7 | Organisational Practices - Incorporate the values of global, social and environmental responsibility into organizational practices.

The Future Starts Now: Enhancing the Global System for Current and Future Generations Through SDGs

After decades of insufficient policy action and environmentally destructive conduct, the triple planetary crisis poses an unprecedented threat to human rights, including those of future generations.

International law, the overwhelming majority of regional treaties and National constitutions recognize today the right to a clean, healthy and Sustainable environment.

Two years ago, the UN General Assembly recognized this right and its role in contributing to the full enjoyment of all human rights, for present and future generations. Environmental rights and other human rights have a critical role to play, ensuring more inclusive and effective policy-making and steering us towards greater justice and peace by ensuring societies where both people and nature can thrive. Grounding the outcomes of the Summit on these rights is essential to correct course and set the path towards greater justice within and between generations, including by accelerating and funding the rapid, full, fair, and effective phaseout of all fossil fuels and ensuring a just and equitable transition to Sustainable economies.

Chapter 3

Curriculum

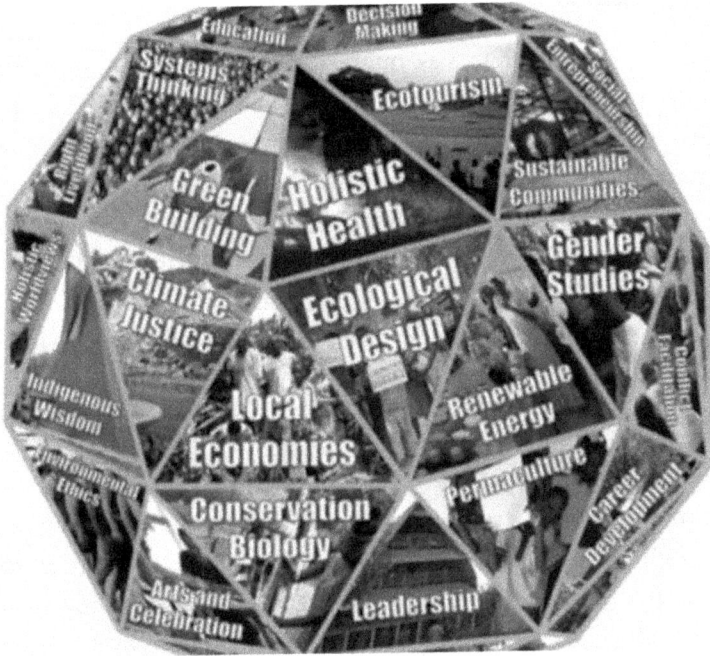

Changing Minds

For most of human history, being a good student of the environment was the difference between life and death. For hunter gatherers, and later for small-hold farmers, close observation of nature was the foundation for productive foraging and hunting, or a decent crop yield. The biologist E.O. Wilson has theorized that for this reason, people have evolved the capacity for an instinctive fascination with the natural world, called biophilia or love of nature. People who were close observers of the natural world, he argues, would be more likely to survive, have children and pass along their genes. So evolution has hard-wired us with the ability to connect powerfully with the nature, and gain a profound pleasure in this close interaction. But just having this capacity does not mean it is exercised. Given this, the theory of change in Environmental Education is simple: awaken students' innate biophilia. Cultivate a love of the natural world through close engagement with it.

Humans no longer live as hunter- gatherers or small-hold farmers. Today more than half of the world's population lives in cities; everyone spends more and more time indoors and online. As most humans no longer hunt or fish or farm for a living or even for recreation, we now desperately need environmental Education, and environmental educators. In an age of accelerating Climate Change and accelerating species extinction, creating an ecologically literate population will continue to be the difference between life and death, now for whole communities. Only by cultivating love and respect for nature will we build powerful political and economic movements to change the rules, change the game, and create a Sustainable future.

In most countries around the world, environmental Education is not a significant part of the public school curriculum. Instead, that role has typically been filled by non-profit organizations who offer in-school, after-school or summer-school programming, and by farms, science centres and museums. In the US, many towns and cities have an active ecosystem of NGO's working to fill this role. Typically, these programs feature project-based learning where students are encouraged to get dirty playing with worms or planting gardens. As students get older, these experiential learning opportunities increasingly focus around solving local sustainability challenges: recycling or climate action. Place-based learning is another hallmark of environmental Education, where students integrate the natural history and ecological functioning of a place with an understanding of the social and historical context of local environmental and social issues. A variant of place-based study, outdoor Education often focuses on developing leadership skills and competencies through team-based experience in nature. The intellectual heart of environmental Education is the idea of ecological literacy: understanding the interactions of complex, biogeochemical systems. And learning as well how human communities engage with these systems.

Equipping Young People

"We have the opportunity to go further than ever in helping citizens, and especially young people, to understand Climate Change, play their part in tackling it, and to become equipped with the skills needed for a Sustainable economy."

Climate Change is a Global issue with local solutions. Vulnerable groups are disproportionately affected by Climate Change. Education equipped with knowledge of Climate Change empowers communities to build resilience and prepare for climate-related disasters, ultimately saving lives.

We want to go further and faster on climate Education – integrating climate content into all stages of learning. This will equip young people with the skills to tackle the climate crisis and become active participants in building a more Sustainable future.

Proposal- Remodel Degrees around SDGs, not Disciplines. Interdisciplinary degrees focused on sustainability challenges would excite undergraduates more than discipline-led courses. If this be the case then Education for Sustainable Development (ESD) will empower students of all ages with knowledge, skills, values and attitudes to address the interconnected Global challenges we face, including Climate Change, environmental degradation, biodiversity loss, poverty and inequality.

1. Ensure learning and skills support school-to-work transitions

- Make Education relevant to the changing forms of work: Alongside other goals, learning must be relevant to the changing world of work. Provide young people with support upon Educational completion to be integrated into different kinds of labour markets – including care economies, entrepreneurial economies, labour markets and the voluntary sector.

- Expose students to different occupations: Industry and community leaders must be better brought into secondary and higher Education to ensure that students are exposed to the world of work and a range of occupations.

- Provide for experiential and lifelong learning: Provide technical and vocational Education and training (TVET) that integrate opportunities for relevant, high-quality, work-based learning. Educational institutions should provide career counselling, foster and support lifelong learning opportunities. Reorient Education to build environmentally Sustainable futures

- Elevate Sustainable development in curricula: Sustainable development should be elevated as both a guiding purpose and organizing principle for curricula, permeating all subject areas while simultaneously cutting across disciplinary boundaries.

- Develop pedagogies to engage with local realties: Support place-based, environmental, outdoor, and experiential Education, and citizenship Education that foster Sustainable relationships with the planet.

- Strengthen literacy, numeracy, scientific capacities: Build knowledge and skills to understand and innovate creative solutions and counter misinformation by teaching students to investigate phenomena through scientific method, rigor, empiricism, and ethics.

- Emphasize 'green skills': Qualifications, programmes, and curricula should deliver 'green skills' throughout life, whether these be for newly emerging occupations and sectors – or for sectors undergoing transformation for the low-carbon economy.

- Ensure Climate Change Education is gender-responsive: Recognize the unequal impacts of environmental destruction on women and girls, and the steps needed to increase the value of domestic and care work in every household and community.

- Assist students to adapt to changing conditions: In communities already feeling the destructive impacts of Climate Change, Education should equip students with emergency responsiveness, impact mitigation, and other capacities to manage the "new normal" of their environments.

- Recognize the role of indigenous knowledge: Welcome and restore indigenous knowledge vital to the mitigation and adaptation to social, economic, and environmental change – such as Sustainable forest management, water sowing and harvesting, biodiversity and crop resilience, seed conservation and selection – and that take an expansive view on the relationships between humans and non- humans.

2. Expand the right to Education throughout life

- Direct higher Education and training towards long-term knowledge and skills: At higher levels, Education should instill people with sophisticated knowledge and cognitive skills. Education systems can gear these capabilities towards enabling people to produce long-term social and economic well- being for themselves, their families, and their communities. •
Remove barriers for access to higher Education and vocational training: Governments and higher Education institutions should alleviate social, cultural, and financial barriers that

prevent access to higher Education, or that saddle students with lifelong debt.

- Ensure the right to early childhood Education: Ensure adequate and sustained public funding for quality early childhood Education to promote the learning, growth and development of all children from birth, which can help to close future learning gaps later in life.

- Equalize high quality instruction at all stages of Education: Prioritize high-quality instruction in the most underserved sectors and population, for example by providing pathways for teacher recruitment from within marginalized populations and providing special supports for novice and experienced teachers in schools with high rates of inequality and attrition.

3. Role of Education for Sustainable Development

Taking a life-long learning approach starting from pre-primary to adult Education, ESD aims to equip all learners with critical competencies covering not only knowledge, but also social and emotional awareness and actions, including critical thinking and collaboration.

With such knowledge, skills, values, and attitudes, learners gain insight into the complexity of the climate crisis, interconnectedness of Global sustainability challenges, as well as how to contribute to problem- solving in daily contexts.

Drawing upon ESD's holistic approach to learning, the Greening Education Partnership by UNESCO aims to inspire action from countries to empower learners with the skills required for inclusive and Sustainable economic development within the context of the transition towards digital transformation.

Drawing upon ESD's holistic approach to learning, the Greening Education Partnership aims to inspire action from countries to empower learners with the skills required for inclusive and Sustainable economic development within the context of the transition toward digital and green economies. It focuses on 4 action areas.

- Greening schools" -- From early childhood through adult Education, work to ensure that all schools achieve green school accreditation, including teacher training and higher Education institutions.

- Greening learning" -- Embrace a life-long learning approach that integrates climate and environmental Education into school curricula, technical and vocational Education and training, workplace skills development, teaching materials, pedagogy, and assessment.

- Greening capacity and readiness" -- Support teachers and policy makers through the integration of climate Education in pre-service and in-service teacher training, building the capacity of school leaders and key Education stakeholders.

- Greening communities" -- Engage the entire community by integrating climate Education in life-long learning, in particular through community learning centres and learning cities.

- We acknowledge that this Global Policy - Education for Sustainable Development (ESD) is just one articulation of a feeling that is being felt all across the world. We see this Policy as one branch of a much wider, stronger, wiser movement and this will include Greening TVET Education also thereby providing green skills for green Jobs for a Green economy.

4. **Technical and vocational training is often unjustly neglected by Education system -** Employers have long been warning of widening gaps between the skills in demand and those that workers actually have - while governments have touted a

need to foster more technical talent if countries want to be globally competitive. One report published by Deloitte estimated that 2.4 million positions in the manufacturing sector alone could remain unfilled between 2018 and 2028, with a potential economic impact of $2.5 trillion. Without adequate modifications to Education and training systems, this gap will only worsen. Closing it promises to only become more complex, as skills requirements change at an accelerating pace - particularly in emerging technology fields. This calls for greater collaboration between the public and private sectors - in particular more needs to be done to better balance the goals and desires of policy makers, politicians and Educational institutions with those of entrepreneurs and investors. There is a better need to understand the linkages between these sometimes-disparate interests, and ways they can be combined to serve people, the environment and broader economies in healthier and more complementary ways.

In 2019, Germany introduced a National continuing Education strategy based on a more holistic culture that takes into account the interests of the government, industry and trade unions- and employs algorithmic matching, financing and the visualization of competencies. Accurate, timely career guidance can help successful transition young people from their school years to employment, by ensuring that they understand their true options based on real labour market data and demand. Proactive career guidance can also help circumvent the gender stereotyping and socio-economic opportunity gaps that often hold young people back from choosing certain occupations. In general, technical and vocational training is underutilized - and often unjustly neglected by Education systems as a second-best option. Such training and Education can be a key driver of economic growth, by providing many of the skills required for jobs that will have genuine staying power in future labour markets. Technical qualifications may be best designed through collaboration between employers and industry groups, and particular attention should be paid to fostering their evolution based on sets of mutually agreed upon standards.

5. **Skills for Work and Life** Technical and Vocational Education and Training (TVET) connects Education and the world of work. TVET aims to address economic, social and environmental demands by helping youth and adults develop the skills they need for employment, decent work and entrepreneurship. In this way, TVET promotes equitable, inclusive and Sustainable economic growth and supports transitions to green and digital economies.

Since the Third International Congress on TVET in Shanghai 2012, TVET has been gathering momentum and Global attention. This increased with the adoption of the Education 2030 Agenda which devotes considerable attention to technical and vocational skills development with specific targets related to access, acquisition of relevant learning outcomes and elimination of gender disparity.

The new UNESCO Strategy for Technical and Vocational Education and Training (TVET) was adopted during the 214th session of the Executive Board for the period 2022 to 2029. Under the theme "Transforming Technical and Vocational Education and Training for Successful and Just Transitions", the Strategy will build upon the achievements under the Strategy for TVET 2016-2021 and seek to generate Global momentum in support of TVET, contributing to the post-COVID-19 social and economic recovery and to an acceleration of progress towards Sustainable Development Goal 4. It will seek to instil a renewed ambition for TVET in Member States and build a common vision for transforming labour markets, economies, and societies. This Strategy is fundamental for its aim to respond to the relevant needs of Member States and the changing demands of TVET.

The UNEVOC Network is the key driver for mutual learning, capacity-building and advancing International cooperation in TVET. As well as UNESCO and its networks, the Members of the Inter-Agency Group on TVET are conducting collective initiatives and joint work to unleash the potential of TVET to meet skills needs of individuals, enterprises and societies.

In context of the above TVET Report by UNESCO UNEVOC let us in brief discuss a case study about how India can gain from its positive demographics, the skill gap must be bridged. Corporates can help by aiding the govt's efforts. India is one of the youngest nations with the average Indian being 28 years of age; the average Chinese is 37 years and the Japanese 48 years. Of the nearly 135 crore Indians (in 2021) around 34% (46.42 crore) were below 19and nearly 56% (75.16 crore) between the age of 20 and 59. By 2041 this demography will change but with 59% of its population between 20 and 59, India could be the world's largest pool of human resource.

To convert this pool into human capital will require steadfast focus on skilling and Education. Over the next two decades, the labour force in the industrialised world is expected to decline by 4%, while in India it will increase by nearly 20%. India could become the supplier of talent and skills if its workforce across age groups is equipped with employable skills that keep pace with the exponentially changing technological ecosystem.

The PLI (Production linked incentive) scheme implemented in 2021 with an outlay of Rs 1.97 lakh crore across 13 sectors have the potential to create National manufacturing champions and generate employment opportunities for the country youth. However, for sustained success , the scale of the skilling effort both for the entrant workers and even more importantly for the existing workforce would be vital. It is only by rasing the skills of its existing workforce, that India will be able to meet its aspirational development goals.

To complement government efforts, systemic corporate investments in skilling could play a decisive role in attracting larger investments at the National level. Corporations could consider industry level collaborations to provide industry specific skills. This would be a CSR investment with a substantial social return, while adding to the availability of quality manpower for their respective sectors. During this decade, India Inc. can play a catalytic role in increasing the availability of skilled manpower in the country.

6. **VET and the Green Transition: What are the skills and Education needed for finance professionals to play their part?**

Managing the impact of people on the planet we call home, has become the rallying call of our times. As governments around the world are seeking to define a vision for decarbonising their economies and achieving net zero emissions, there is an urgent need for all stakeholders to grasp the scale of this challenge and to respond to it. In too many organisations however, expertise in climate risk and ESG still resides in a small group of sustainability experts; this must change rapidly and become embedded in organisations' culture. There is a pressing need to raise the level of knowledge and understanding, both to recognise Climate Change as an urgent 'burning platform' – and to respond accordingly.

Finance professionals and professional accountants have a critical role in putting sustainability at the heart of decision-making, and in championing responsible practices that will drive the critical changes the planet needs, both to lead long-term value creation within Sustainable economies, and to champion responsible practices in the public interest. And to make sure they have proper tools at their disposal to do so, they must be equipped with the right Education and skills.

The Time for Action is Now

Governments, companies and individuals have to come together to address the urgent climate crisis. Policymakers, business leaders and the Global workforce have a shared opportunity and responsibility.

Achieving our climate targets is a monumental task and it is going to take a whole-of-economy effort to make it happen. That means we need a transformation in the skills and jobs people have if we're going to get there.

Green skills are the core of the green transition and harnessing the shift of talent. Through a targeted approach, we can progressively shift towards these greener jobs, using skills to identify jobs with the highest ability to turn sectors and countries green. We need more opportunities for those with green skills, we have to upskill workers who currently lack those skills, and we need to ensure green skills are hardwired into the skillset of future generations.

A petition calling for mandatory, fully integrated climate literacy Education, civic skill building, and jobs training so that everyone can participate in the creation of an equitable green economy and this should have Organisations including - teachers' union, labor unions, faith groups, mayors, corporations, Governments, tech companies and NGOs along with individuals across the planet. A final document that does not explicitly include these issues will not prepare our students for the impacts and opportunities presented by the climate crisis. The future will not be the same Post COVID 19. We know that for certain. Let us Care about the Future of God's Creation - Our very own Planet Earth.

Section I - Shifting Paradigms: Fostering Sustainable Lifestyles and Rethinking our Relationship with Nature

Currently Responsible for around 75 per cent of Global CO2 emissions, cities – and in particular the transport systems and office buildings – play a pivotal role in the world's response to the climate crisis. In addition to being central to the transformation to inclusive and green economies, cities are also at the forefront of efforts to empower local communities with the knowledge and skills that are needed to break long-established patterns of unsustainable consumption, production and mobility. To instil climate consciousness and equip local residents with the green skills essential for a Sustainable society.

Fostering Sustainable lifestyles and rethinking our relationship with nature. Whether greater emphasis is paid to cycling to work or school, engaging in conscious consumption or being mindful when sorting waste, reflecting on how we can live more sustainably plays an important role in addressing Climate Change. In this context, there is a pressing need to develop a new ethical foundation for humanity's relationship with nature.

Below Mentioned Principles Adds a Climate and Sustainability lens to the Curriculum

Principle 1- Opportunities are needed to build awareness of the interconnected nature of social injustice and the ecological crisis. Questions Environmental justice.

Principle 2- Systems thinking is essential to help students to appreciate the interconnectedness of living and non-living elements of the biome including complex and non-linear interactions in time and space including within the human world itself

Principle 3- Sustainability is a moral question that is value-laden and therefore political and plural. Amendments should recognise that there is no universal definition or application of sustainability and provide opportunities for different priorities in relation to sustainability to be revealed.

Principle 4- Sustainability is an interdisciplinary and transdisciplinary matter meaning that students will encounter it interpreted differently in each subject they do. Links to other disciplines, especially between Arts and Sciences should be identified.

Principle 5- An awareness of eco-anxiety is critical - it needs to be acknowledged and its potentially negative impacts on learning and wellbeing should be confronted.

Principle 6- Our curriculum should engender a sense of awe and wonder both in nature and in human ingenuity. Students should have opportunities to learn about the ways in which humans are working with and through nature to solve complex issues.

Principle 7- Learning must support students to develop capabilities and dispositions for action. This will mean different things in different subjects but will often involve student-led action on locally relevant issues, working with others including local community experts.

Principle 8- Encouragement of creative and critical thinking, as well as an understanding of - and preparedness to confront - uncertain futures, should be foregrounded wherever possible; this requires caution bearing in mind Principle 5.

Principle 9- Learning in/as/for/through the environment can be transformative but is more often than not about more modest, incremental changes so curriculum amendments should address both these possibilities. This Principle is also about outdoor learning and calls for opportunities for outdoor learning of different kinds and for different purposes to be incorporated.

Principle 10- Opportunities are needed to allow for unforeseen learning e.g. emerging from the community and from pupils' own questions and needs from the community, the pupils and their questions/needs and others. Space for community engagement and pupil-led debate needs to be encouraged.

Investing in Transformative Educators, Curricula and Content, Pedagogies Based on SDGs:

Investing in educators means supporting their professional development, socio-emotional and physical safety and well-being, and ensuring they have appropriate knowledge and skills to teach about SDGs. are also questions of social justice and amendments should seek to highlight this where possible.

Ensuring quality Educational content, including curricula and digital and analogue teaching materials, supports learners and teachers, Education administrators and managers, and other stakeholders to examine, challenge and change attitudes (based on SDGs that harm individuals, society, environment and prosperity. Place equity and relevance at the core of Educational transformation, considering contemporary challenges across all subjects to develop the knowledge, skills and values that will help everyone reach their fullest potential, interact with others respectfully, and engage meaningfully with their environment while building social, economic and environmental sustainability.

Using participatory, relational and collaborative pedagogies stimulates a love of learning and creativity; builds technical and critical literacies; and supports equity, health, inclusion, innovation, peace and Sustainable consumption. Teaching that is technology-led or from instructional scripts is less successful at building the skills and competencies required for transformative change.

Fostering positive relationships between teachers and learners, teachers and parents, and schools and homes supports cognitive development and learning, and socio-emotional well-being for all. Positive school-community relationships allow schools to become hubs for intergenerational learning and community-building. International, regional and local collaborations among all Education stakeholders promote learning and knowledge exchange, along with values of openness and equity. Pre-service teacher training should include such positive relationship-building; in-service mentoring can also contribute to fostering positive school environments.

How lifelong learning can be harnessed to promote Sustainable consumption, the use of green mobility, responsible waste management and an appreciation of natural resources. How family learning, Indigenous knowledge systems and strengthened urban-rural understanding can foster Sustainable living and, ultimately, redefine humanity's relationship with nature.

Lifelong Learning for Climate-Action - to build people's capacities in five key areas –leadership, project management, resource mobilization, leave no one behind and communications - to support them in climate-related projects

- Devise an inclusive climate action project or initiative that contributes to Global efforts to tackle Climate Change.

- Outline a brief communications plan to promote climate-friendly projects and initiatives.

- Identify the resources needed to successfully implement a climate project or initiative.

- Describe key elements to consider when conceptualizing and implementing inclusive and gender-responsive climate projects and initiatives.

- Make use of different leadership styles in climate action projects and initiatives.

How Climate Change Knowledge can Become Action

Reviews the core skills, values and actions as well as knowledge that are required for transformative Climate Change Education that will bring about social change.

Objectives and Key Questions

A holistic curriculum and pedagogy that engages across cognitive, socio- emotional and behavioral dimensions is necessary in developing learners who are knowledgeable, competent, skilful and engaged in taking climate action. However, an analysis of country submissions under the United Nations Framework Convention on Climate Change note that cognitive learning is more commonly discussed in relation to Climate Change Education than social and emotional or behavioural learning, regardless of Education level. Similarly, an analysis of Educational plans and curricula frameworks in close to 50 countries across all regions note the lack of attention to socio-emotional skills and action-oriented competences that are central to sustainability action.

It is important that Education policies, curriculum and pedagogies go beyond focusing on the cognitive knowledge and engage learners in their hearts and hands to lead profound changes in our societies towards sustainability.

- What needs to be integrated into curriculum to empower learners as agents of change towards the climate crisis. The session will address the following questions:

- What knowledge, skills, values, and action need to be enhanced in Education policies and curriculum to ensure learners are empowered to address the climate crisis?

- How can learning about Climate Change be translated into action for Climate Change?

Education for Post-Carbon Green Economies

Structural transformation towards post-carbon green economies and a 1.5-degree lifestyle, as well as how knowledge, skills, values and actions relevant to economic transition can be integrated into Education policies and curricula.

Objectives and Key Questions

The evidence of the climate crisis, the limits of natural resources, the impact of pollution and the growing inequalities and social injustice, shows that reconciling economic growth with the principles of Sustainable development is challenging as long as current industrial and production models, built to pursue unlimited economic growth, continue. Therefore, in a post- carbon green economy, a systematic redesign is needed to radically transform the way we build our economies. According to the report of the Intergovernmental Panel on Climate Change (IPCC), limiting Global warming to 1.5°C would require 'rapid and far- reaching' changes in all sectors of society and the reduction of Global net human-caused carbon dioxide emissions by about 45% from 2010 levels by 2030, reaching 'net zero' around 2050.

A transition towards a post-carbon green economy, which implies meeting the needs of all people without overshooting earth's planetary boundaries, requires fundamental rethinking of all aspects of our societies. Concrete changes in lifestyles are also integral to the solution for a Sustainable future. The 1.5-degree lifestyle questions current consumption patterns and promotes strategies to achieve low-carbon lifestyles. With this in mind, knowledge, values, attitudes, and actions need to change at both the systemic and individual level. Education encourages this paradigm shift by raising awareness of the structural changes and promoting alternative values, such as fairness and solidarity, away from the notion of unlimited economic growth.

Furthermore, Education fosters competencies such as civic and political engagement, so people can engage directly in the political and advocating process, while also equipping learners with the skills that will be required in future jobs created by the 1.5°C transition.

What needs to be integrated into Educational policies and curricula to help accelerate the transition to alternative Sustainable economic models and promote individual Sustainable lifestyles.

- What is the role of Climate Change Education to promote the transition towards a post- carbon green economy?

- How can Climate Change Education foster a 1.5-degree lifestyle?

Now or never: Adapting Teaching and Learning in a Changed Climate

Reflects on our new realities shaped by the inevitable consequences of Climate Change. Within this context, the curricula should examine the teaching and learning that are needed to help learners adapt and live in the changed climate, including the importance of social and emotional learning.

The Ancient Futures: Un-Learning and Re-Learning our Way Towards a Post-Carbon Future

Discuss the values and practices of harmony embedded in traditional knowledge and indigenous communities across the world, and how they help us visualize a post-carbon future. Good practice stories should be shared to inspire a brighter future for collective efforts fighting against Climate Change.

Learning for Life: Transforming Education for a more Sustainable Workforce.

In a fast-changing world, it is more important than ever to rethink the purpose, content and delivery of Education to keep up with the demands of the workforce.

How Education systems can be transformed to develop the current and future workforce, enabling them to thrive as resilient leaders of Sustainable transformation.

- How can curricula be developed to equip learners with the skills and knowledge to lead and advocate for inclusive, Sustainable development? What skills need to be nurtured and recognised and why?

- How are employers harnessing professional development and capacity building to promote and develop skills related to sustainability, gender equality and social inclusion within their workforce?

- How can employers and Education providers best align efforts to ensure lifelong learning and Sustainable skills development?

- How can we ensure that Education strategies effectively translate to business and a wider cultural transformation?

Interdisciplinary Strategic Actions to Accelerate Sustainable Urban Development

Cities represent the future of Global living and they play a pivotal role in achieving climate neutrality. Research and innovation and actions on zero-emission mobility, positive clean energy, urban greening and re-naturing are some of the strategies that cities will need to address. Teacher Education should highlight:

- Research and innovation case studies to support Sustainable urban planning

- Smarter cities: How integrating innovative approaches can achieve a more liveable and environmentally Sustainable city environment and support economic growth

- How to establish a robust and innovative monitoring framework to track the progress and effectiveness of future strategies

Research and innovation for Sustainable and Equitable Access to Education

Education technology has experienced exponential growth in recent years. However, the speed at which it has been developed and embedded into learning environments has meant that more in-depth research and development approaches were often neglected. This oversight has led to cost inefficiencies, low impact and even exacerbated gaps in equity of access to Education. how research and innovation stakeholders can evolve to align their practices to generate tangible improvements in Education outcomes for all.

- How are different stakeholders employing innovative tools such as big data and analytics to identify and close gaps in Education access? Can these approaches be improved and, if so, how?

- How should research communities and solution providers develop practices and approaches to address gender- based barriers to equitable Education access?

- How can Education providers work with researchers and solution providers to drive evidence- based innovations that can be meaningfully embedded into teaching and learning?

Supporting Strategic Development Across the UN's SDGs for Institutions

With the next generation of students placing great emphasis on sustainability, it is becoming essential for the world's higher Education institutions to demonstrate a commitment to a greener, fairer, more equitable society.▯

THE' SDG Academy–can help institutions build expertise in using the UN's SDGs and THE's Impact Rankings to demonstrate social impact.

- Overview of the SDG Academy and the potential benefits to institutions, academics and staff who work on sustainability strategy, data collection, measurement or communications • Practical advice on developing a sustainability strategy for institutions using data and insights

- Learn how to effectively showcase your institution's impact on society and demonstrate stewardship of resources and outreach within local communities

Harnessing Education and Gender Equality for Sustainable Development

Education is a fundamental necessity to ensure a prosperous, just and equitable society. However, women and girls continue to be marginalised, with 40 per cent of countries still lacking gender parity in primary Education, resulting in restricted access to skills development and limited employment opportunities for young women. This session will foster an outcomes-focused dialogue to recognise how different stakeholders are working to close the Global

Education equity gap and improve learning and livelihood outcomes for all.

- What are the main barriers to accessing quality Education? How are cross-sector stakeholders working to overcome these?

- What challenges currently exist in breaking down gender-based barriers to Education access?

- To what extent are sectors collaborating to shift towards a culture of gender equality and ensure women and girls' full participation in Education, employment and society? What does success look like and what still needs to be done?

How can we Integrate and Sustain Green Skills within Life-Long Learning?

Lifelong learning is intrinsically linked to Sustainable development in several ways, affecting Education, the workforce, gender equality, climate action and more. This discussion will uncover the benefits of integrating sustainability skills into lifelong learning, and how building a climate-literate workforce can help us progress towards a more Sustainable future.

Scaling up Climate Change Education Post COP27

Reviews the gaps, challenges and opportunities in promoting Climate Change Education for social transformation in Education and Sustainable development policies and curriculums. The discussions presented concrete strategies to promote the greening of every Education policy and curriculum, particularly around and after COP27.

Post-COP27 Climate Change Education: Where do we go from here and its key takeaways, achievements, and commitments made related to Climate Change Education.

Section II - Pedagogy

Bridging the Digital and Green Transitions"

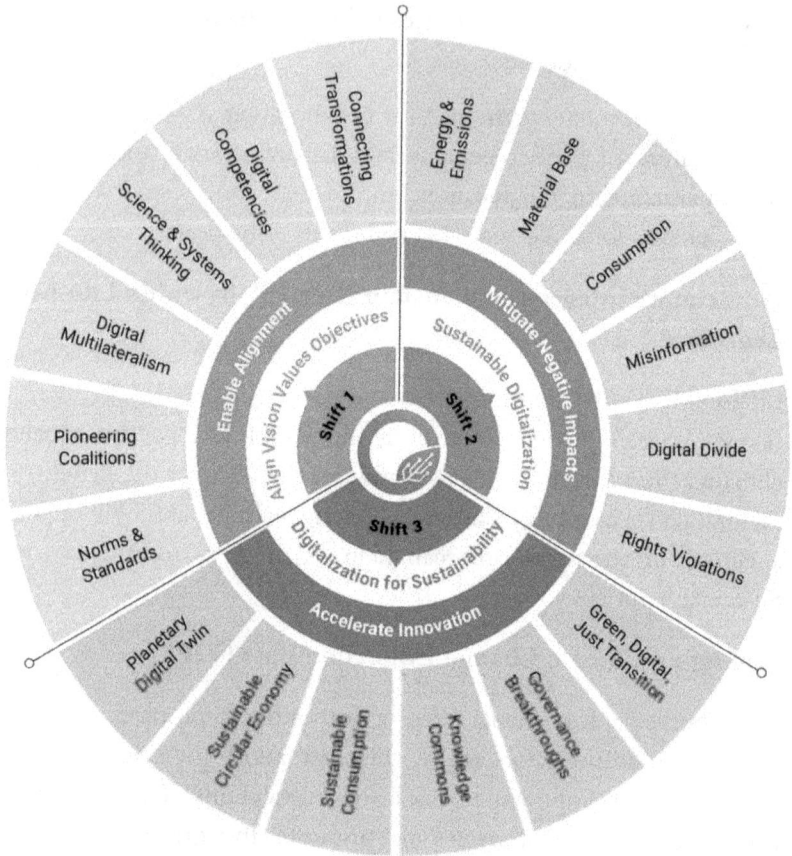

The urgency of the green transition cannot be overstated. Despite growing awareness and calls for action, we continue to push the climate and natural environment to withstand new extremes of strain. While the green transition struggles to gain momentum, the digital and AI transition is fully underway

With Climate Change, the digital transition poses significant challenges to Education and is forcing us to rethink traditional pedagogical practices, curriculum design and even the purposes and aims of schooling.

As the digital transition of Education expands and accelerates, countries around the world are working to determine how it can be steered and regulated to ensure it facilitates greater inclusion, quality and equity in Education. But questions of how this transition affects sustainability are largely overlooked.

Expanding Sustainable Solutions Through AI and Digital Technologies

AI and digital innovations have the potential to revolutionise and accelerate the delivery of the SDGs.

These technologies can improve data collection, analysis and communication, empowering communities to make more informed decisions, adapt to changing environments and implement scalable solutions.

This track will explore how cutting-edge innovations in AI, data analytics and digital technology are driving solutions for Global challenges, from climate action and healthcare to Education. Industry leaders will come together to share their latest developments, consider the ethical management of AI and develop strategies to ensure that all communities benefit equally from these advancements.

Below roadmap outlines new data, evidence, and examples on how countries can harness Education to propel climate action. It provides an actionable policy agenda to meet development, Education, and climate goals together, recognizing that tackling Climate Change requires changes to individual beliefs, behaviors, and skills – changes that Education is uniquely positioned to catalyze.

How Education can link the green and digital transitions to support a Sustainable and prosperous future, with four concrete ideas for action.

Four ideas that provide a roadmap to leverage technology in Education –

Idea #1: Tech to Deepen Our Understanding of Climate Change

First, we need technology to help understand Climate Change through multimedia and interactive digital tools. By providing a platform for both knowledge dissemination and dynamic engagement, digital technology can be an ally in building awareness about sustainability and equipping learners with the skills and understanding needed to take action to rebalance our relationship with the climate and natural environment.

Idea #2: Tech for Experiential Learning to Promote Climate Action

By using technology to facilitate hands-on experiences, schools and communities can deepen understandings of sustainability and empower students to adopt environmentally responsible behaviours. What is clear is that technology has vastly expanded the Educational toolkit for deepening our understanding of Climate Change. Interactive simulations, dynamic maps, multimedia storytelling and immersive VR experiences –all made possible by digital tools– help students and the wider public better comprehend and better appreciate dynamic climate systems, the factors driving Climate Change, and potential future scenarios depending on actions or inactions taken to mitigate the production of greenhouse gases. Importantly, these learning experiences go beyond presenting dry scientific facts; they connect students to issues by localizing them and showing how they are influenced by government policies. By supporting knowledge dissemination and better tailoring content for individuals, classes, schools and communities, digital technology can be an ally in building awareness about sustainability and equipping learners with the understanding needed to rebalance our relationship with the nature and environment.

Idea #3: Tech to drive Green Energy Research and Innovation

Technology, in general, and AI, in particular, are instrumental in driving research and innovation to promote green energy solutions. Technology optimizes renewable energy sources like solar and wind, advances climate adaptation strategies, supports Sustainable agriculture, and enhances waste management, among many other uses.

Idea #4: Tech to Cultivate Green–Digital Global Citizens

When used thoughtfully and critically, technology is a powerful and versatile tool for Global citizenship Education. However, to harness this potential, Education must prioritize approaches that integrate digital literacy, sustainability, ethical participation, creativity and emotional intelligence.

This will help learners develop the mindset and skills needed to bridge the green and digital transitions. As the 2030 deadline for achieving the Sustainable Development Goals approaches, Education provides the means of connecting the Global digital transition with the green transition that we – and the natural world upon which we depend – so urgently need.

Some other approach to implement Sustainable Development Goals –

- Local-to-Global Connection
- Community Climate Action Network across the globe demonstrates how Global climate issues can be translated into local, tangible concerns like changing weather patterns
- The connection between countries in the Climate Justice resource shows how climate impacts and solutions cross borders

- Multiple Learning Approaches

- The resources use diverse formats (websites, podcasts, toolkits, PDFs) to reach different audiences

- They combine practical tools with Educational content • The 'Inform, Investigate and Instigate' model provides a clear framework for moving from understanding to action • Emphasis on Deliberative Democracy

- The Global Community Assembly Toolkit particularly stands out for its focus on collective decision- making

- It promotes inclusive dialogue about finding "fair and effective" solutions

- Intersectionality in Climate Action

- The Climate Justice resource explicitly connects climate issues with broader social justice concerns like –

  - Food and water security

  - Healthcare access

  - Educational equity

  - Gender justice

  - Racial justice

  - Focus on Practical Action

  - These resources aren't just theoretical - they provide concrete tools for community engagement

  - The emphasis on "having your voice heard" around COP events shows the importance of civic participation

o Finally, and perhaps most important, we must equip a new generation of Global citizens with the knowledge, skills, attitudes, and behaviours to confront today's interconnected challenges, including Climate Change.

How Universities can work towards the SDGs How Higher Education Institutions are advancing efforts to overcome Global Challenges

Worldwide Universities Network consortium launches 'Tertiary Education in a Warming World' Report. It says –

Higher Education institutes have a critical role to play in driving the scientific, political, technological, and cultural change needed to avoid the worst-case Climate Change scenarios, and in advancing the societal adaptive capacities needed to meet the ongoing challenges posed by the ongoing environmental crises.

In response to the intensification of the environmental problems, growing numbers of institutes of higher Education are declaring climate emergencies and making public commitments to supporting and contributing to the realisation of Global environmental and social goals. Further, many dedicated individuals working in the sector are already driving meaningful action through rigorous research, teaching, knowledge sharing, and public engagement. There is a growing consensus that sector- wide change is needed to ensure that aspirational declarations and positive individual actions translate into Sustainable and transformative change.

To contribute to such efforts the Worldwide Universities Network (WUN) Education in a Warming World Research Consortium is launching the Tertiary Education in a Warming World report. It is intended to be a resource to other academics and policymakers who are also grappling with promoting a robust Climate Change and sustainability agenda within tertiary Education. The report illustrates a number of trends, examples, and reflections on how third-level

Educational institutes can work towards creating a more Sustainable future. Drawing on Tristan McCowan's framework, the research group focuses on five modalities of third-level institutional operations, to provide an analytical lens to understand better the complex interplay between higher Education institutes, societies, and Climate Change. Specifically, they focus on the following dimensions:

- **Education:** The importance of highlighting the powerful structural forces driving the crisis, and engaging in empowering classroom practice

- **Knowledge Production:** Engaging diverse perspectives and pedagogies, including Indigenous knowledge systems, and arts-based approaches

- **Service Delivery:** Providing Climate Change Education to professionals across various sectors

- **Public debate:** How third-level Educational institutes can support academics to engage in climate advocacy

- **Campus Operations:** Whole-systems approaches to greening the campus and engaging in sustainability initiatives in local communities

The research consortium situates their reflections within this framework as a helpful structure that considers the multiple dimensions of institutional action, builds on it, and engages with it by considering relevant literature and case studies from the universities that form the Education in a Warming World research consortium

Sustainable University Leadership and Governance towards the 2030 Agenda

Higher Education institutions play a fundamental role in the training of future professionals, responding to Global challenges and a changing world. International, governmental and Sectoral agreements have accorded on this challenge and committed to support the transition towards university sustainability, identifying mobilizing actions to be undertaken in order to ensure quality Education, to collaborate in reducing the degradation of the natural environment, to promote regeneration, ecosystem care and the permanence of humanity.

To encourage students to become agents of change who have the knowledge, the means, the will and the courage to take transformative actions towards Sustainable development, Educational institutions must transform themselves. Therefore, the institution as a whole needs to be aligned with the principles of Sustainable development, in order to reinforce their learning content and pedagogies by the way in which facilities are managed and decisions are made internally. This holistic institutional approach to Education for Sustainable Development requires learning environments in which learners learn what they live and live what they learn.

- What should be the priorities for higher Education sustainability and how do we implement them on our campuses given the urgency of the times?

- How do we catalyze the higher Education community to overcome barriers and accelerate the scaling of Climate Change solutions?

- What do YOU need to support you in this work?

It is necessary to identify a roadmap that allows the authorities and the entire university community, to carry out good practices oriented to their materialization and measurement, through actions that are clearly aimed at achieving the promotion of the SDGs and thus comply with the 2030 Agenda.

To reflect on their strategic plans and deepen their collective awareness aimed at promoting a Sustainable culture. The experience will be aimed at developing a space for dialogue and exchange of knowledge and best practices and thus deepen what is Sustainability, what is Education for Sustainable Development, as well as the signing of an institutional agreement to achieve the commitments contained in the 2030 Agenda.

A Model of Social and Collaborative learning can be developed, strengthening the network of Universities for Sustainability.

Objectives can be –

- Guide University governing bodies in understanding the opportunities offered by the SDGs and what steps should be taken to implement them to meet the 2030 Agenda.

- Provide knowledge and solutions that support the implementation of the SDGs at the university.

- Incorporate the principles of the SDGs through governance, management and university culture.

- Learn about conceptual and methodological frameworks to promote the SDGs within the university and the 2030 Agenda

- Identify and analyze good practices carried out by other universities in the areas of training, research, institutional management and university extension.

- Encourage peer-to-peer learning and cooperation on sustainability issues.

- Contribute to the design of an Implementation Plan as a roadmap with solid activities aimed at achieving the commitments made in the 2030 Agenda and incorporating the SDGs into the university's strategies, policies and plans.

The final result will be a roadmap for measuring the scope of actions in relation to the SDGs and its Implementation Plan for the Strategic Sustainable Project at the University.

1. Sustainability at the heart of University Strategy

The development of a need for a fairer and more inclusive world. Therefore, this module on Sustainable culture requires a clear awareness that it will focus on developing a space for dialogue to deepen what is Sustainability, what is Education for Sustainable Development, the 2030 Agenda with the SDGs, the relationship with stakeholders and material issues.

Objectives:

- Establish the importance of sustainability as a transversal articulating axis in the strategy of HEIs from the ESD framework.

- To delve deeper into the SDGs and the value of universities in achieving them.

- Develop a change management framework with agile methodologies to identify material issues and stakeholder engagement.

- Align the strategy with the National regulatory framework of University Social Responsibility, Rights and obligations.

2. Accelerating the SDGs in Universities

Addressing the challenges of the SDGs requires new knowledge, new ways of doing things, making difficult choices between contrasting options and, in some cases, profound transformations. This module provides a clear vision of how universities can contribute to the implementation of the SDGs through their own functions: Education, research, action and social leadership.

Objectives:

- Conduct a self- diagnosis of the activities carried out at the university itself itself using the RESIES tool

- Recognize strategies to integrate sustainability in a transversal way in teaching, research, innovation and extension in order to contribute to the 2030 Agenda.

- Understand the importance of stakeholder engagement, communication and dissemination in order to contribute to the SDGs.

- Learn about inspiring cases: integrating sustainability into HEI strategy.

3. Governance and Sustainable Leadership

A sustainability initiative implies major transformations, common to the activities of a higher Education institution. These require a strong institutional commitment, as well as governance structures that enable the effective participation of the institution's various stakeholders and the coordination of sustainability efforts.

Objectives:

- Analyze how high-level strategies, policies, plans and reporting indicators align with the SDGs and identify which organizational units are relevant to each other.

- Incorporate the SDGs as a result of conscious integration with the strategies, structures, status and specific challenges of each university to generate value in society.

- Strengthen the strategic development plan with sustainability from a conceptual framework for the implementation and contribution to society from the 2030 agenda.

- Recognize the importance of monitoring and measurement that contributes to decision making and value generation for all stakeholders.

4. Challenges and Pathways to 2050

Universities are often large entities and can have a significant impact on the social, cultural and environmental welfare aspects within their campuses, communities and regions, and sometimes far beyond. These impacts relate directly to all areas of the SDGs and by acting responsibly universities can make significant contributions to their achievement. Leveraging their unique position within society, universities, both individually and collectively, can help lead, guide, and support local, National, and International responses to the SDGs.

Objectives:

- Identify the main opportunities and challenges in the training of tomorrow's leaders and today's citizens

- Reflect on the trends in higher Education and the paths towards 2050.

- Integrate the value of strategic alliances and knowledge networks.

- Global Network ESD for 2030

5. Higher Education for Sustainable Development (HESD)

As the world continues to face multiple crises, including pandemics, stakeholders must prioritize Sustainable futures for young people. This means equitable access to basic Education, relevant skill building and a focus on green jobs and green economies.

Higher Education should work on cross-Sectoral partnerships ensuring that children and youth have access to quality basic Education and relevant skills that can help achieve all Sustainable Development Goals.

This can Happen by

- Bringing together stakeholders to discuss actions to fill gaps in Education / employment programming for Sustainable employment for young people

- Help in Identifying foundational skills needed for young people to thrive in 21st century green economies, and to build Sustainable lifestyles, environments, and cities,

- Spotlight the role of quality basic Education, gender equality, and decent work in building Sustainable cities and communities, and

- Discusses the role of all stakeholders including private sector, Civil society, Government, Business, NGOs etc to collaborate with young people and take a future forward

- Provide a platform for young people to meaningfully engage in a dialogue with UN Member States and UN entities on transformative pathways for realizing Sustainable development.

- Share knowledge, skills, and lessons learned in achieving the rights and well-being of youth by promoting the accelerated implementation of the 2030 Agenda and ensuring the meaningful participation and engagement of young people in policymaking and implementation.

- Present ideas and solutions -- and showcase innovative initiatives and individual and collective action by youth and others -- to advance the SDGs based on National, regional and Global experiences.

- Discuss and report on progress for the implementation of the UN Youth Strategy, Youth 2030: Working with and for Young People, and other issues related to young people including sharing information on plans for measuring and monitoring its impact at the country, regional and Global levels and considering the role that young people and youth organizations can play in the implementation of the strategy.

The Higher Education Universities Forum can provide a platform for young people to engage in a dialogue with Member States and other actors to voice their views, concerns and galvanize actions on how to transform the world into a fairer, greener and more Sustainable place guided by the Sustainable Development Goals (SDGs).

What does the Higher Education sector need to do in order to respond to the challenges of Climate Change? Educators and leaders are already driving impact in their schools and communities — embracing evidence-based solutions, innovative practices, and an emerging consensus around Education as a key lever for climate action and equity. How can we broaden that vision and scale that impact?

Why a 21st-century civic Education needs to include climate Education. Educators can prepare students with the knowledge, skills, and perspective to face Climate Change through responsible citizenry. As Climate Change continues to disrupt our world— from agriculture and energy to health and National security—teachers can keep students empowered and hopeful by activating the classroom with solutions-based approaches and action-oriented opportunities.

- Understand why making climate connections in civic courses helps build hope and resilience for students.

- Explore free, non-partisan, ready-to-use simulations and lesson plans on Climate Change and an Earth Month Calendar of activities to engage your students.

- Discover a Climate Civics Toolkit to build activities into the classroom experience.

Driving Universities' Core Business towards SDGs and Sustainability

Universities play a crucial role in addressing and promoting the United Nations' Sustainable Development Goals and sustainability. Five leading partners like higher Education institutions, the private sector, International organisations and granting agencies with regard to the role that can play in advancing sustainability including:

- Education – curriculum integration, interdisciplinary approach, experiential learning

- Research – innovative research, International collaboration, knowledge transfer

- Policy advocacy – expertise/recommendations, stakeholder partnership and public engagement

- Campus operations – Sustainable practices, carbon neutrality and Education/engagement with stakeholders within the university

"Education is going to be critical for SDG solutions."

In any theory of change, especially in the area of climate, "a piece of that has to be Education of our youth, Education of our youngest citizens — helping them understand, in a very constructive way, how the world is changing and how they can be part of having that change be something that's going to be OK for them. That's an incredibly important challenge for everybody."

"Climate Change isn't just about warmer temperatures. It's about the potential loss of stability. In a less stable world, we're going to need a new skill: climate awareness. We need to be aware of the world around us. We need to bring the physical world into our lives." These are pressing issues at the intersection of Education and climate - "Climate

Change is not a future problem; Climate Change is already happening, and it affects us all,"

Let us showcase how we can and should rely on universities to teach and research while elevating the thought leadership of today's college and university students.

Higher Education should conduct research on the psychological, cultural, and political factors that influence environmental attitudes and behavior; teaches students; informs and engages the public through environmental journalism; and supports a Global network of organizations seeking to build public and political will for environmental solutions.

What Next?

Education can make an important contribution to sustainability but for it to truly deliver, major change is needed.

At a philosophical level, the magnitude of what faces humanity requires a more comprehensive eco social framing of the sustainability challenge: one which encapsulates both Climate Change as a Global phenomenon and environmental issues as a more immediate and localized manifestation. We must concurrently address greenhouse gas emissions, the unSustainable use of resources and degrading of natural systems on which we rely.

Bringing the sustainability focus of Sustainable Development Goal target 4.7—to ensure all learners acquire knowledge and skills needed to promote Sustainable development by 2030—requires moving beyond knowledge to developing agency and empowering for action. Such a shift cannot be achieved by curriculum alone. More attention is needed on pedagogical approaches and assessment that value, measure and incentivize agency as well as greater consideration of who are the 'agents' of change: teachers, students and parents.

The challenges are, however formidable. Foundational learning levels are abysmal and access to secondary Education, limited. Transformative Education is reliant on a well-prepared, supported and motivated teaching workforce which can't be assumed to always be in place. Further, it should be expected that an increased incidence of extreme weather events will further erode learning time. Between 2022 and 2024 alone, 404 million students across 81 countries experienced school closures with an average loss of 6% of the academic year.

As the 2030 deadline for achieving the Sustainable Development Goals approaches, I am convinced that Education offers an essential bridge connecting the Global digital transition underway with the green transition that we – and the natural world upon which we depend – so urgently needed.

Section III - Sustainability Skills

"We know that Education is critical to empower young people with the skills, knowledge and understanding needed to understand the root causes and consequences of Climate Change and prepare them to find solutions and to thrive in our changing world."

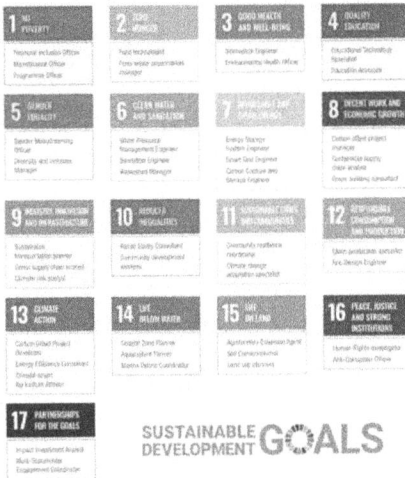

ESG ROLES
TO ACHIEVE THE SDG GOALS

SUSTAINABLE DEVELOPMENT GOALS

Aligning our Education systems with the needs of our planet is essential. Programs and curricula must reflect the realities of our ecological crisis and the requirements of a green economy. Initiatives such as the 'International Green Learning & Skills Accelerator' are crucial in plugging this gap by bringing different stakeholders together. The commitment of educators, policymakers, and industry leaders: will be the driving force behind this transition. I urge you to prioritize this alignment. Invest in green skills Education. Support policies that facilitate continuous learning. Create pathways for young people to enter and thrive in green jobs. Nothing good ever happens in isolation;

the urgency of this collaboration is even more evident today. Therefore, by working together, we can shape policies and initiatives that guarantee a smooth and fair transition for all, creating a just and Sustainable society where no one is left behind.

Skilling Youth on the Move to help power the Green Economy

Skills are a key factor in the economic development of countries and the prosperity of nations. Countries, regions and sectors therefore require skills-matching mechanisms, instruments and policies to reduce the gap between the supply and demand for skills in the labour market, increase the employability of the workforce and reduce skills shortages. Where macro-economic policy-making is concerned, Sectoral approaches strengthen good practices in skills development by putting the emphasis on the skill-sets needed in different economic sectors, rather than taking a generic approach.

To help participants better understand the characteristics, methodologies, institutional arrangements, skills governance mechanisms, and Sectoral skills development modalities needed for identifying labour market imbalances in terms of skills development at a Sectoral level, in addition to recognizing the current and future skills needed at a Sectoral level in a broader macro-economic policy framework.

'Green transitions'—shifts in economies towards more Sustainable practices that preserve, restore, and protect the environment—have the potential to create 8.4 million jobs for young people by 2030. But 'youth on the move' are often left out of policies and programming aimed to support young people's participation in the green economy. Overlooking this group perpetuates their marginalization and ignores the diverse perspectives and innovative ideas they bring to green economic transitions, leaving a large pool of talent untapped.

How can Educators Fast-Track Green Skills Opportunities for Students?

Sustainability and green skills are becoming increasingly necessary for the future of work; so higher Education institutions must fast-track the teaching of these skills, to match their growing demand. Policy makers must address the importance of Education-corporate partnerships and effective curriculum programming. Explore how to increase climate literacy and green networking opportunities among students.

How are Emerging Leaders Practising Green Skills?

Current and future generations will become the leaders responsible for driving efforts towards a more Sustainable future. Explore how today's emerging leaders can implement and develop green skills throughout their careers to create long-lasting positive and meaningful impact. Explore how academia, business, government and civil society can better support emerging leaders through improved communication and collaboration.

AI – Friend or foe to Green Skills?

While we become more aware of the challenges posed by AI to Education, it is vital that we also focus on the possibilities offered by technology, in terms of progressing Sustainable development. This dichotomy in relation to the green skills agenda and examine the utility of AI-Education partnerships in moving towards a knowledge economy, underpinned by sustainability principles and an exploration into the AI-green skills nexus.

How can we Integrate and Sustain Green Skills within Life-Long Learning?

Lifelong learning is intrinsically linked to Sustainable development in several ways, affecting Education, the workforce, gender equality, climate action and more.

Uncover the benefits of integrating sustainability skills into lifelong learning, and how building a climate-literate workforce can help us progress towards a more Sustainable future.

Section IV Sustainability Workforce

Climate Workforce or Sustainability Career Through Sustainability Skills

T-Sustainability Professional
Breadth of experience, knowledge, and skills

United Nations agreements such as the 2015 Paris Climate Agreement are giving Education policy an unprecedented role of significance in catalyzing public support for climate action. This research project examines influences on the development and direction of UN policy programs related to Climate Change communication and Education (CCE). These influences include policy actors such as National and subnational governments, NGOs, academic institutions, think tanks, foundations, corporations, and other actors from civil society; as well as the meetings, meetings infrastructures through which they interact with UN policy programs.

Building skills friendly cities is essential to creating the local ecosystems to prepare our youth the skills necessary to fill jobs for the future and meet growing industry demands by 2030. Data demonstrates that youth across the world are not being prepared in sufficient numbers with the Education and skills necessary to obtain a living wage job and start on a career pathway. Although there are regional differences, there is room for improvement for all cities across the globe.

For countries to thrive economically, cities must address this future skills gap and invest more in developing youth skills now. This means increasing access to early childhood programming including pre-kindergarten, boosting graduation rates, creating workforce training and employment programs for opportunity youth, and ensuring living wages for youth, among others. Cities must work in partnership to develop policies and programs that equip young people with the skills necessary to obtain jobs quality jobs that not only meet growing industry demands but also provide a living wage and a career that allows for economic mobility.

We would like cities to ask themselves how they rank when it comes to pre-K enrollment, opportunity youth, youth wages, graduation rates, city median age? Ask yourself what you can do if you are a youth leader or a leader in city government, K-12 and higher Education, or even a non-profit. How can you work in partnership with community leaders and youth to ensure the economic vitality of cities and allow its young people to thrive? At the very least, every stakeholder can work to adopt the standards that we set forth, create community partnerships, engage youth in the planning process, and work to increase access to the vital skills, credentials, and employment opportunities that set cities on the pathway to success.

Supporting Strategic Development across the SDGs for Institutions

With the next generation of students placing great emphasis on sustainability, it is becoming essential for the world's higher Education institutions to demonstrate a commitment to a greener, fairer, more equitable society. through the Global Goals to demonstrate social impact.

- Potential benefits to institutions, academics and staff who work on sustainability strategy, data collection, measurement or communications

- Practical advice on developing a sustainability strategy for institutions using data and insights

- Learn how to effectively showcase your institution's impact on society and demonstrate stewardship of resources and outreach within local communities

How can Emerging leaders practice Green Skills?

Current and future generations will become the leaders responsible for driving efforts towards a more Sustainable future. Explore how today's emerging leaders are implementing and developing green skills throughout their careers to create long-lasting positive and meaningful impact. We will also discuss how academia, business, government and civil society can better support emerging leaders through improved communication and collaboration.

Training the responsible Leaders of tomorrow: Engaging and Upskilling Employees for a Sustainable Future

Learning does not stop in the classroom; it is vital to ensure that we can adapt and develop our skillset to meet the evolving needs for Sustainable development. This panel will examine how leaders and organisations can meaningfully and strategically invest in building people's capacity to ensure a resilient, empowered workforce and society.

- Positive approaches to sustainability leadership. How can leaders motivate and empower employees to drive Sustainable actions in business?

- What does authentic employee engagement look like?

- How can we instil a culture of lifelong learning at a policy, industry and institution level?

Digital Solutions for a Sustainable Future Workforce

In the wake of unprecedented disruption from the Covid-19 pandemic, the purpose, content and delivery of learning have been radically reimagined across formal Education, professional development and lifelong learning. This panel will highlight how digital technologies can be harnessed to upskill and reskill the current and future workforce, equipping them with the tools needed to drive Sustainable development.

- How can technology best drive impactful learning and capacity-building initiatives? What has worked well and what could be improved?

- How can employers use technologies such as AI to create personalised, equitable learning experiences and development pathways?

- How can Education institutions and employers harness technologies such as micro credentials to foster lifelong learning in the current and future workforce?

How do Universities lead Democratic, just and Cultured conversations to support Global Sustainability?

Polarised views and controversy dominate community and societal dialogue, directly affecting the daily lives of students, academics, staff, supporters and stakeholders. Our communities look to higher Education institutions to support public dialogue on diverse issues such as artificial intelligence, Climate Change, climate justice, environmental degradation, freedom of expression, academic freedom, equity and inclusion, misinformation, disinformation and the Global events that put these issues at the forefront of public attention.

The Promises and Challenges of Green Skilling in Global context

This keynote will offer a Global perspective on the promises of green skilling and highlight the obstacles that we must collectively overcome as we transition to net zero. We will discuss how the Global workforce can be successfully upskilled and reskilled in line with National sustainability targets. Specifically, this session will touch on the role of higher Education institutions in promoting the green agenda among younger generations.

Interdisciplinary Strategic Actions to Accelerate Sustainable Urban Development

Cities represent the future of Global living and they play a pivotal role in achieving climate neutrality. Research and innovation and actions on zero-emission mobility, positive clean energy, urban greening and re-naturing are some of the strategies that cities will need to address. This session will highlight:

- Research and innovation case studies to support Sustainable urban planning.

- Smarter cities: How integrating innovative approaches can achieve a more liveable and environmentally Sustainable city environment and support economic growth.

- How to establish a robust and innovative monitoring framework to track the progress and effectiveness of future strategies

Fostering advocates for Sustainable Cities and Communities: The Role of Education and Training

The transformation of cities requires a new set of Sustainable skills and a shift in mindset. Through Education, training and campaigns, cities can foster citizens' awareness of the importance of green transition and contribute to shaping a new generation of environmentally responsible consumers, employers and employees. Explore :

- How to employ cross-sector training and development programmes for the current workforce
- Creating advocates for Sustainable solutions on urban development and communities
- Shaping strong partnerships to develop policies and academic programmes aligned with promoting Sustainable urban development
- How to strengthen Educational programmes in urban planning and Sustainable design and thinking

Navigating Biodiversity Initiatives: What to do next for Conservation Progress

Through real-world case studies - organisations can seize opportunities to implement effective, collaborative, value-creation strategies on biodiversity and nature to explore –

- The strengths and gaps in current biodiversity collaborative conservation initiatives
- How organisations can adopt nature-based solutions, and supporting and incentivising Sustainable food and agricultural practices

A Collective effort on Research and Innovation towards Global Restoration of Biodiversity

The Global restoration and conservation of biodiversity is essential for a Sustainable future. Frameworks for International research coordination and cooperation are in place, but are they working? What else do we need?

- What innovative resources and strategies are we using to advance biodiversity conservation?

- The transition from lab to real life: How do we translate research and innovation into real-life biodiversity restoration initiatives?

- The role of research and innovation in engaging broader society in conservation efforts

Bridging the Knowledge Gap on Biodiversity Systems

Innovative Educational strategies are needed to foster an environmentally conscious next generation of citizens and employees. Delving into behavioural and cultural shifts, will take a holistic look at the linked dynamics between food systems, land use and biodiversity.

- How can we implement Educational initiatives to ensure the next generation of citizens and employees are environmentally aware?

- How are businesses and civil society empowering the current and next-generation workforce to foster Sustainable practices?

- What behavioural and cultural changes are required to successfully implement Educational initiatives?

Building a Workforce for a Low-Carbon Future

Low-carbon economies can be achieved only by implementing strategies that build strong leadership, enhance the right skillsets and foster workforce ownership dedicated to achieving a low-carbon world. This panel will highlight how employers and Education providers can collaborate to nurture a resilient, carbon-literate workforce that can power a more Sustainable future.

- Include diverse voices to solve diverse problems: Understand how to identify talent pool gaps and enhance Sustainable transition leadership roles in the corporate world

- How can Education providers and employers best collaborate to design and implement capacity-building programmes that will enhance knowledge and skills related to Sustainable practices?

- How can organisation leaders ensure and empower employees' ownership and commitment to the organisation's sustainability journey?

Powering a Greener Future: Global Strategies for a Sustainable Energy Transition

Long-term, strategic planning is essential to enable transition to the use of greener and more Sustainable energy sources. How different sectors can work together to create and implement strategies to transform industry and move towards decarbonised energy systems at a global, regional and local level.

- What are the main barriers to achieving energy transition and how are they being addressed

- Frameworks and guidelines development: What are International organisations and standard-setting bodies doing to help businesses transition?

- How are businesses embracing sustainability practices as a long-term viability and competitiveness enabler?

- How are we approaching energy security and ensuring stability in the face of economic and geopolitical challenges ?

- Transformative change: from advancing renewable energy to creating millions of green jobs that fuel economic prosperity. With the right training and tools, we can empower communities worldwide to thrive while protecting our shared home.

Catalysing Sustainable Business Transformation through Research and Innovation

Research and innovation are key to developing solutions for an effective, Sustainable and just energy transition at both speed and scale. How to best approach and harness research and innovation to explore new energy sources and navigate scalability challenges, while mitigating the impacts of Climate Change and sustainably improving energy security.

- Understand why R&D necessitates a multidisciplinary, multisectoral, portfolio approach

- How can we mobilise the innovation capacity of all stakeholders for the greater good?

- How can we leverage monitoring, modelling and analytics tools in tracking sustainability goals to foster evidence-based decision-making for a greener future?

- What innovations and tools are enabling tangible impact and progress in the Sustainable energy transition and why? What can we learn from their development and implementation?

Examine trending transformative initiatives and showcase the pioneering efforts of leading institutions to integrate sustainability across academia, research and practice. Explore how business schools are not just preparing future leaders, but actively contributing to a more Sustainable and prosperous world.

How are Businesses responding to Local Sustainability Challenges and Inequalities?

Ensuring that the green agenda is equitable and accessible must be prioritised as we transition towards a more Sustainable future. Evaluate the challenges and opportunities in various contexts, considering how different countries and regions use green skills for the wider sustainability agenda, and how businesses can contribute to an inclusive green economy.

Navigating the Intersection of Finance and Sustainability for today's Chief Financial Officer

Nowadays, it is non-negotiable that the drive towards Sustainable development is at the core of every financial decision within an organisation.

So, Explore:

- Why the CFO is crucial in leading sustainability initiatives that deliver long-term value creation and environmental, social and governance (ESG) objectives for organisations

- How to build a strategic and emotionally intelligent approach to collaboration across functions for financing Sustainable initiatives

- Promoting cross-sector collaboration in the pursuit of a more Sustainable and fair future for all

Chapter 4

Lifelong Learning

Figure 1. Competitive Sustainability Compass

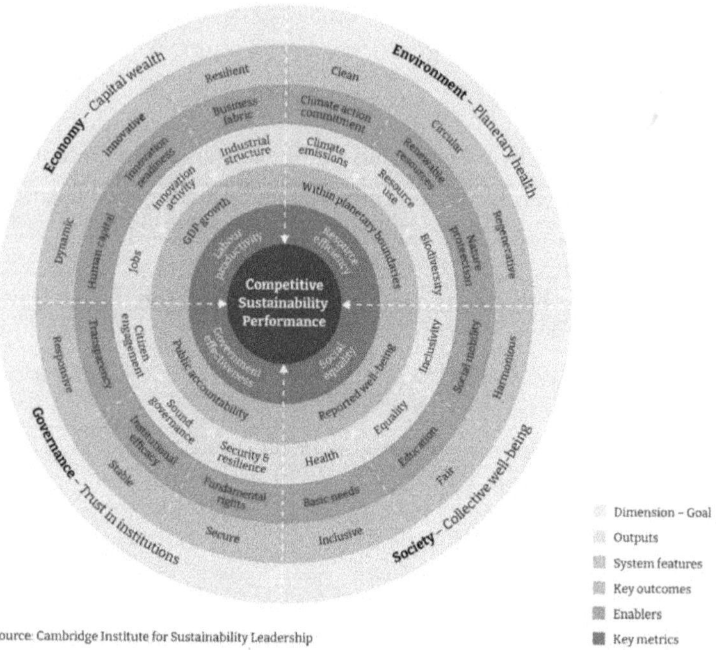

Source: Cambridge Institute for Sustainability Leadership

- Dimension – Goal
- Outputs
- System features
- Key outcomes
- Enablers
- Key metrics

Lifelong learning is intrinsically linked to Sustainable development in several ways, affecting Education, the workforce, gender equality, climate action and more. Uncover the benefits of integrating sustainability skills into lifelong learning, and how building a climate-literate workforce can help us progress towards a more Sustainable future.

Evaluating and Enhancing Progress towards 'Strengthening Education Systems from a Lifelong Learning Perspective' –

Six in ten workers globally are expected to require reskilling by 2027, according to the World Economic Forum's Future of Jobs Report 2024. Global reskilling is an urgent priority to enable green and digital transitions, and to make Global value chains (GVCs) more sustainable. Companies and industries are racing to adopt Sustainable practices across their operations, supply chains, and business strategies. Yet only half of the workforce currently have access to adequate training.

In times of uncertainty and social upheaval, the International community, and specifically, the Member States of the United Nations, remain the main actors for leading the urgent changes the world needs to overcome the crises of our days. Along with seeking immediate solutions to conflicts and disasters, world leaders are called to strengthen the societal foundations essential to advance the realisation of a lasting Sustainable development, capable of ensuring peace, justice, democracy and equality.

While we recognise and support the Human Rights International Framework and the Sustainable Development Agenda, we also stress that progress in their realisation cannot be possible without Education and lifelong learning.

Due to its enabling nature, Education opens the door to realising all human rights since it aims to build people's learning and capacities needed to transform the world. Despite its transformative potential, the realisation of the human right to Education continues to face dramatic obstacles, such as lack of financing, the exclusion of important populations such as girls and children with disabilities, the attacks against youth, teachers, students and schools, and the utilitarian reduction of the curriculum, among many others.

We recognise many States' efforts to meet the Sustainable Development Goals, including SDG4. We also welcome the Summit of the Future, which, far from being an isolated initiative, aligns with the work of the UN Treaty Bodies, the High-Level Political Forum, and the recently undertaken Transforming Education Summit and SDG Summit. In these initiatives, it has become clear that whatever the paths of Sustainable development are, it will be very difficult to transform Global governance in the medium and long term, and even more so, to achieve International peace and security if the structural causes are not addressed through Education. Education and lifelong learning are not an end in themselves but the basis of Sustainable development.

Behavioural nudges for Climate Change are strategic techniques designed to influence and encourage people to make more environmentally conscious decisions without forcing them.

Here's a comprehensive breakdown:

✓ Comparison Mechanisms

- Team Comparisons - Foster healthy competition between groups to achieve sustainability goals

- Self-Comparison - Track personal progress over time for continuous improvement

- Average Benchmarking - Measure performance against community standards

- Leaderboards - Motivate through friendly competition and recognition

✓ Rating Systems

- Star Ratings - Simple, intuitive 3-tier evaluation system

- A-B-C Grading - Clear performance classification that drives accountability

✓ Feedback Tools

- Real-time Feedback Loops - Immediate response systems for behaviour modification

- Character Gauges - Visual representation of progress

- Ambient Data Display - Public environmental metrics

- Color-coded Systems - Intuitive visual cues

- Progress Tracking - Clear visualization of advancement

✓ Progress Monitoring

- Interactive Tracking - Gamified progress visualization

- Star Charts - Achievement documentation

- Geographic Mapping - Spatial progress tracking Implementation Levels

- Progressive Difficulty (1-10) - Structured advancement path

- Tiered Challenges - Customized difficulty levels for varied engagement

✓ Commitment Strategies

Public Pledges - Community-visible commitments

- Private Goals - Personal accountability measures

- Gradual Engagement - "Foot in the door" technique

- Multi-Day Challenges - Sustained behavior change program

Despite this, we see with concern that Education is not properly addressed in the scope of the Summit of Future and its draft Pact for the Future, lacking the necessary strength to structurally promote, from the bases, the changes the world needs. A future without Education is a return to the past!

The Futures of Education

POSSIBLE FUTURE DISRUPTIONS

Overview

ENVIRONMENT
Hothouse earth: *Crossing climate tipping points fuels an environmental catastrophe*
Silent spring: *Cascading extinctions threaten vital ecosystem services*
Sea-level rise: *Flooding and storm surges threaten lives and livelihoods*
Heat waves: *Too hot to live*
Climate despair: *Climate change exacerbates a global mental health crisis*

SOCIAL
Conspiracy chaos: *Misinformation and disinformation paralyse democracy*
Cruelty-free society: *Societies call for animals and ecosystems to be considered active policy stakeholders*
Indigenous reimagining: *A grassroots-driven rethinking of values and institutions*
Green radicalisation: *Protests escalate in response to stalled climate action*

TECHNOLOGY
Biotech breakthrough: *The fusion of biology and digitalisation transforms the economy*
Cyber slowdown: *The dark side of digitalisation leads to an economic downturn*
Artificial intelligence leap: *Technology brings new tools that transform society*
Virtual worlds: *Most people spend most of their time in highly immersive virtual reality*

ECONOMY
Well-being economies: *Taking a more holistic view of societal success*
Accelerated convergence: *The African economic miracle expands the global middle class*
Environmental-industrial complex: *Wartime spending on climate action*
Crypto century: *A blockchain boom follows a crypto winter*

GREEN TECH
Green tech failure: *Tech shortfalls necessitate larger behavioural shifts*
Transparent environment: *Real-time data increase environmental accountability*
Captured carbon: *Carbon capture alters the climate-policy landscape*

GEOPOLITICS
Tech titans: *Private companies displace governments*
Regional conflicts: *Military spending increases as multiple conflicts fester*
Divided world: *Global co-operation falls amid superpower competition*
Multitrack world: *A reversal of globalisation and increased regionalisation*
Rising authoritarianism: *Anti-democratic leaders undermine global collaboration*

Our world faces complex disruptions, unique opportunities and uncertain futures. How must Education rise to the challenges ahead – not only to react but to help shape the future?

Our world is at a unique juncture in history, characterised by increasingly uncertain and complex trajectories shifting at an unprecedented speed. These sociological, ecological and technological trends are changing Education systems, which need to adapt. The climate crisis, the pervasive rise of Artificial Intelligence, growing inequality and societal divisions are compelling us to reconsider our approaches. Indeed, we face an existential choice between continuing an unsustainable path or radically changing course. But no trend is destiny. It is urgent to imagine new future possibilities.

Education is crucial to this change of course. It has great potential to help shape more just, inclusive and Sustainable 222futures by rebalancing our relationships with each other, the living planet and with technology. Yet, to do so, Education itself must be transformed.

Yet Education has the most transformational potential to shape just and Sustainable futures. UNESCO generates ideas, initiates public debate, and inspires research and action to renew Education. This work aims to build a new social contract for Education, grounded on principles of human rights, social justice, human dignity and cultural diversity. It unequivocally affirms Education as a public endeavour and a common good.

Education and learning systems are at a critical juncture. The climate crisis, the pervasive rise of Artificial Intelligence, growing inequality and societal divisions compel us to rethink the role of Education in shaping shared futures. We face an existential choice between continuing an unsustainable path or radically changing course. But no trend is destiny. There is an urgency to shape alternatives and reimagine possible futures. Education is crucial to this change of course. It has great potential to help shape more just, inclusive and Sustainable futures by rebalancing our relationships with each other, the living planet and technology. Yet, to do so, Education itself must be transformed.

However, the Education paradigm cannot rely solely on knowledge transfer but needs to focus on social and emotional, and action-oriented learning." The power of the collectives includes the power of teachers, youth, policymakers, and researchers. Many stakeholders are now engaged in various dimensions of Education for Sustainable Development, including Climate Education, Environmental Education, Green Education, and Global Citizenship Education. Many countries have committed to Target 4.7 in their policies and curricular practices. However, many challenges remain in implementation.

Five priority action areas outlined in the ESD for 2030 Roadmap are :

- Advancing policy

- Transforming learning environments

- Building capacities of educators

- Empowering and mobilizing youth

- Accelerating local level actions

Questions and points to be reflected include –

- What are some of the collectives in Global Education at the Higher Education level working on regarding green curriculum, systems thinking approaches, and institutional and infrastructural greening?

- What are teacher collectives that teachers would like to join and get inspiration from? What are some opportunities for Global teacher professional development?

- Collectives are needed for curriculum development k-12 and beyond? Who is in the space, and what are they creating?

- NGOs are superstars! They create some amazing programs that connect the hardest to reach.

- Non-formal and informal educators need to share the limelight to share strategies.

Technological Advancement is rapidly reshaping the World of Work. But what are the trends to keep an eye on?

- As businesses rethink workforce strategies, those that prioritize talent innovation will lead the future of industrial transformation.

- By 2030, more than 20% of jobs are expected to transform due to disruptions in the labour market. A new Forum report introduces a five-step framework for public employment services to enhance job matching to get workers into meaningful roles.

- The Forum's 2025 Future of Jobs Report highlights the transformative changes reshaping the job market and the skills driving these shifts. This video explores which jobs are growing the fastest, why these roles are thriving and what skills are most essential in tomorrow's workplace.

Why it matters: Technological change, geoeconomic fragmentation, economic uncertainty... many drivers are shaping and transforming the Global labour market. It's up to leaders to implement workforce transformation strategies in response to these shifts.

Choosing our Future - Education for Climate Change Education is a key asset for climate action. Education reshapes behaviors, develops skills, and spurs innovation— everything we need to combat the greatest crisis facing humanity. Better educated people are more resilient and adaptable, better equipped to create and work in green jobs, and critical to driving solutions. Yet, Education is massively overlooked in the climate agenda. Almost no climate finance goes to Education. Channeling more climate funding to Education could significantly boost Climate Change mitigation and adaption. At the same time, Climate Change is a huge threat to Education. Millions of young people face lost days of learning because of climate related events. In low-income countries the situation is worse. Unless made up, this lost learning will negatively impact their future earnings and productivity. It will also lead to great inequality both within and across countries. Governments can act now to adapt Education systems for Climate Change.

Key-Takeaways:

- The economic losses and human cost of Climate Change are enormous. Despite this, climate action remains slow due to information gaps, skills gaps, and knowledge gaps.

- Education is the key to addressing these gaps and driving climate action around the world. Indeed, Education is the greatest predicator of climate-friendly behavior.

- Better educated people are more resilient and critical to spur innovation and climate solutions. An additional year of Education increases climate awareness by 8.6%.

- Education can empower young people with green skills for new jobs, but also augment skills for existing jobs.

- Education is massively overlooked in climate financing and Climate Change is threatening Education outcomes.

- Climate-related school closures mean students are losing days of learning. Even when schools are open, students are losing learning due to rising temperatures.

- Governments can take steps to harness Education and learning for climate action by, for example, improving foundational and STEM skills, mainstreaming climate Education, and building teacher capacity. And governments can prioritize green skilling and innovation in tertiary Education to help supercharge a shift to more Sustainable practices.

Education is the key to bringing the digital transition into better harmony and confluence with the green transition.

The digital revolution can – and must – empower students to:

- Deepen their understanding of Climate Change;

- Engage in experiential learning to take climate action;

- Drive green energy research and innovation; and, perhaps most importantly,

- Emerge as Global citizens.

An Education focused on these goals will shape a new kind of citizenship – one that is committed to harnessing the power of digital technology to activate and drive the green transition.

Education can propel faster and better climate action in two crucial ways. First, Education can galvanize behavior change at scale - not just for tomorrow, but also for today. Second, Education can unlock skills and innovation to shift economies onto greener trajectories for growth.

At the same time, Education needs to be protected from Climate Change. Extreme climate events and temperatures are already eroding hard-won progress on schooling and learning. Climate Change is causing school closures, learning losses, and dropouts. These will turn into long-run inter-generational earnings losses putting into jeopardy Education's powerful potential for spurring poverty alleviation and economic growth. Governments can act now to adapt schools for Climate Change in cost-effective ways.

Safeguarding biodiversity and improving natural resource management Sustainable management of the world's natural resources and food systems is crucial for preserving biodiversity, maintaining ecosystem health, providing resources necessary for human survival, and sustaining a balanced relationship between nature and development.

This Education track can address the intersection of nature, biodiversity, food systems, water resources and oceans. It can bring together leaders from academia, government, industry and NGOs to share insights on innovative research, cross-sector partnerships and practical solutions for safeguarding ecosystems, enhancing food security, improving water management, building finance and fostering climate resilience.

Partnerships for long-term Sustainable urban development

Cities accommodate more than half of the Global population and, by 2050, more than 2.5 billion people will be added to the world's urban population. The success of many of the SDG goals depends on effective cities and communities, as they promote inclusive growth, reduce environmental impact and ensure access to resources and opportunities for all.

This Education track can focus on creating a foundation for long-term Global development, asking how governments, private sector organisations, academic institutions and civil society can address urban challenges with sustainable, inclusive solutions for funding, policy, governance, planning and equitable service delivery.

Expanding Sustainable Solutions through AI and Digital Technologies

AI and digital innovations have the potential to revolutionise and accelerate the delivery of the SDGs. These technologies can improve data collection, analysis and communication, empowering communities to make more informed decisions, adapt to changing environments and implement scalable solutions. This track will explore how cutting-edge innovations in AI, data analytics and digital technology are driving solutions for Global challenges, from climate action and healthcare to Education. Industry leaders will come together to share their latest developments, consider the ethical management of AI and develop strategies to ensure that all communities benefit equally from these advancements.

The Importance and Strategies of ESD in Responding to the Era of Climate Catastrophe

Combating Climate Change Across Generations: Reinforcing Global to Local Policy Action for Education

In our interconnected world, Climate Change affects all of us. Within K-12 Education, 80 percent of administrators and teachers want to teach about Climate Change but do not feel knowledgeable enough to do so. If educators are equipped to teach about Climate Change, they can inspire the next generation to take climate action.

Action is needed: From International Policies to Local Actions

The climate crisis needs to be confronted from various angles, ranging from International policies to local actions. The International response is key to developing a comprehensive game plan to safeguard a just future for all of humanity through universal strategies and goals.

The key to driving effective, lasting change on climate and sustainability issues is collaboration—across sectors, geographies, and demographics. These resources provide a great starting point, and the more we can share and learn from each other's experiences, the more empowered we become to take collective action.

How to teach through the lens of the Sustainable Development Goals: Bridging the Divide through Digital Education go to website- https://www.sdgreadiness.com

SDG Readiness Platform (SRP) offers insight on how the Global Goals can provide a useful framework to guide students' learning across multiple disciplines. A seemingly irreconcilable paradigms from an integrated landscape approach perspective. We think of landscapes as systems whereby all 17 goals are connected in some way. The SDGs provide a fantastic framework/ Course Curriculum by - mapping the connections and thinking about implementation and progress on targets. No single SDG can be dealt with in isolation; thus, only by addressing them all can true Sustainable development be achieved.

Having an online repository of resources with a strong analytical course framework to address Global challenges keeping all stakeholders in mind like Educators, researchers, Universities, academia, Business groups and Governments through articles, case studies, news reports, theoretical/conceptual paper, research framework, course pedagogy, practical experience etc. has proven useful.

Rooting the resources on the SDGs gives students exposure to real-world issues and problems that they can, and do, explore further. Evidence demonstrates strong correlations between Education and diverse outcomes ranging from health, climate, economic growth and wages to equity, diversity and inclusion. This Platform explores how corporate actions, small and large, can make a quantifiable and direct impact across all aspects of environmental, social and governance (ESG) priorities.

The Platform provides a framework for discussion in Education and Climate Change to mitigate risk, improve corporate performance, government perception. while making a more tangible impact on society.

References

https://www.unicef.org/media/165206/file/SOWC-2024-executive-summary-EN.pdf

https://www.unesco.org/en/renewing-Education-transform-future?hub=81942

https://www.unesco.org/en/climate-change/Education/cop

https://www.unesco.org/en/articles/shaping-resilient-future-reeningEducation-core-cop29

https://www.globalpartnership.org/blog/sustainability-Education-antidote-climate-anxiety-not-just-facts-also-actions

https://www.unicef.org/reports/state-of-worlds children/2024?utm_campaign=SOWC%20statistical%20compendium& utm_medium=email&utm_source=Mailjet

https://www.worldbank.org/en/topic/Education/publication/Educati on-for-climate-action#:~:text=Education%20systems%20can%20empower,%20equip, %20and%20skill%20young%20people%20for

https://www.unesco.org/en/renewing-Education-transform-future?hub=81942

https://www.teachthefuture.uk/tracked-changes-project?link_id=0&can_id=9ea40666e9ff2f56ae5fda840a1dd459&sourc e=email-budget-2024-14bn-for-school-rebuilding-next-year-2&email_referrer=email_2543719&email_subject=curriculum-for-a-changing-climate-is-back

https://wun.ac.uk/article/wun-consortium-launches-tertiary-Education-in-a- warming-world-report/

https://www.gse.harvard.edu/ideas/askwith-Education-forum/22/10/Education-and-climate-action

https:// www.iesalc.unesco.org/en/the-universitys-path-towards-the-sdgs-development-of-the-2030-agenda/https://chatgpt.com/share/67937915- bf8c-8012-b207-00da93878b46

www.globalpartnership.org

en.unesco.org

www.lesalc.unesco.org

www.norrag.org

leadthechange.bard.edu

www.gse.harvard.edu

v.worldbank.org

gbc-Education.org

www.futurelearn.com

www.timeshighered-events.com

Thomas Macintyre, Daniella Tilbury, Arjen Wals. "Education and Learning for Sustainable Futures - 50 Years of Learning for Environment and Change", Routledge, 2024

wun.ac.uk